STRUCTURING
YOUR CLASSROOM
FOR ACADEMIC SUCCESS

Stan C. Paine  JoAnn Radicchi
Lynne C. Rosellini
Leslie Deutchman
Craig B. Darch

Research Press Company
2612 North Mattis Avenue / Champaign Illinois 61821

ISBN 0-87822-228-6   Library of Congress Catalog Card Number: 83-61812

To students everywhere, who ask only for a *real* chance at success in school.

To teachers and administrators everywhere, who need to attend only to these few more details to make themselves and their students more successful in the classroom than ever before.

To Gerald, who opened his classroom to us and showed us what can be accomplished with a group of hard-to-teach students.

To Tuck, our colleague, friend, and teacher.

Contents

Foreword

Structuring Your Classroom for Academic Success is written for the teacher in training and for teachers who would like more guidance in managing their classrooms successfully. Those preparing for practice teaching will also find this book an invaluable guide. It provides an overview of what teaching is all about—focusing on the important management skills every teacher needs and on the details of ensuring that each student has a chance to win in the classroom. The authors' recommendations are based on current empirical research and the experiences of outstanding teachers in elementary education. As such, the text can serve as a valuable supplement to a course in educational psychology, or as the basis for classroom management courses or inservice teacher training programs.

A unique feature of the book's practical approach is the use of scripts that outline specifically how to teach students the various procedures. Ultimately, students are trained to manage their own behavior without depending on the teacher's supervision. The scripts are modeled after the Direct Instructional Approach of Siegfried Engelmann.

Most importantly, *Structuring Your Classroom for Academic Success* is not simply to be read but to be put into practice. While this step requires some commitment from the reader, the investment will be repaid many times over. I highly recommend this book to anyone who is interested in the successful education of children.

College of Education
University of Oregon

Wesley C. Becker
Associate Dean

Acknowledgments

Many people played a part in the preparation of this manual and in the development of the procedures presented in it.

Dave Campbell and Margaret Johnson of the Eugene (Oregon) Public Schools and Doris Horton of the Flint (Michigan) Public Schools were the principals of the schools in which these procedures were tested and evaluated. Their consent and support were critical to the success of the project.

Gerald Walters and Robert Benson of the Eugene Public Schools and Carrie McCree and Mildred Robinson of the Flint Public Schools were the teachers of the field-test classrooms. Their cooperation throughout the project was amazing and gratifying, and they provided us with an enormous amount of input and feedback.

Additional suggestions, reactions, and support were given by Gary Davis, Ed Kameenui, Linda Olen, Jerry Silbert, Leslie Zoref, Peter Sharpe, Lynne Anderson-Inman, and Melissa Hayden, all of the Direct Instruction Project staff.

Ira Aronin, Kathy Higgins, Marie Street, and Teddie Softley collected and summarized the data; Tuck Stevens skillfully trained them and coordinated their efforts.

Doug Carnine provided a highly motivating and supportive environment for all of us in which to conduct this work.

Beth Frosland typed the completed manuscript.

All of these people provided the time and the talent required to complete the project, and they did so in a spirit of professionalism and cooperation. To all of them we extend our sincere thanks.

Eugene, Oregon   Stan Paine (for the authors)
April, 1983

xi

Chapter 1

Introduction

Looking in on a typical morning in Ms. Hansen's classroom, we see her in a corner of the room working on reading skills with a small group of students. While she listens carefully to the students answering her rapid questions about the story, she is also aware of what is going on in the rest of the classroom. She looks up and calls across the room, "Susan, that's the way to work. Brian, you're still working well." As she returns to her task, she notices that Amy, who had been daydreaming, has started working again.

The other students are busy completing their assignments. Ted has a sign up on his desk showing he needs help, but he is continuing to work on some of the extra practice material he was given this morning. In another corner of the room, Walter is practicing arithmetic facts with Mary, the part-time aide.

Two visitors enter the room. Ms. Hansen asks them to take an observation and feedback form from the box by the door, and to read and complete the form as they observe. (An example of the form is presented in Appendix A.) By using the form, the visitors will learn about the classroom without taking up Ms. Hansen's valuable teaching time. They will also be able to give her feedback on how they perceive the classroom.

When the reading group comes to a close promptly at 10:00, the children in the group quietly pick up their chairs and return to their desks. Walter also returns to his seat. The students who have been working at their desks put away their books and papers, quickly getting out their social studies books. By the time Ms. Hansen has picked up her own book and papers for the social studies lesson, the children are quietly waiting for the lesson to begin.

Later in the day, while the whole class works on an arithmetic assignment, Ms. Hansen walks between the desks, stopping to check a few problems for one student, then moving to another. She stops long enough to say, "That's how to work quietly, Roy. Ann, you're working hard," then moves to Bobby's desk, since his sign is up showing he needs help. One of

1

the children's mothers is a volunteer tutor, and she is giving George a short reading lesson in a partitioned part of the room. Nancy and Michael are checking their own work against the answer keys at the checking station. As Nancy finishes, she places her corrected paper in the box for that assignment and returns quickly to her seat.

After the final class period, Ms. Hansen decides to use the last 15 minutes of the day to practice a set of arithmetic problems similar to those the children had trouble with during the day's regular math lesson. She again shows them how to do the problems, then divides the class into two teams and gives each team member a set of several problems. When all the students are finished, the answers are shown on the overhead projector; each student grades his or her own problems. The winning team is announced, and two monitors quickly pick up the papers and give them to Ms. Hansen just before the bell rings. She will take a look at each paper and record the results on the children's individual graphs so they can see their progress tomorrow.

The classroom just described is run according to procedures you can learn from this book. They will help prevent problem behaviors, keep students on-task, and make the best use of everyone's time and energy. These procedures will require extra planning and effort on your part at the beginning of the school year, but will result in better classroom management and higher student performance overall. As the year goes on, many of the procedures can be dropped or shortened as students internalize the new routines.

These procedures not only will benefit you by making it easier to run your classroom, but also will make it easier for the children to learn by giving them more opportunities to see and practice new material. Small-group teaching is encouraged to present concepts at the students' level of understanding and give all group members a chance to participate. Extra practice time for difficult material is scheduled daily through both teacher presentation and individual seatwork.

Pilot Testing of the Procedures

The procedures presented here were evaluated over an 8-month period in a school in Eugene, Oregon. They were first introduced into a pilot classroom, where all the procedures for managing the classroom over a full school day were in effect during most of the testing period. Some of the procedures were also tested in six other intermediate grade classrooms. Each teacher tried a different combination of procedures, but all had positive results.

The pilot classroom was a third/fourth grade combination of 14 children. Most of them were Title I (disadvantaged) students. The teacher had 5 years of teaching experience; a part-time aide with 3 years' experience also participated.

Through a series of after-school meetings and in-class sessions, the teacher was trained by a consultant to use the various components of the classroom system. The organizational components of the program—a revised classroom schedule; classroom rules; the physical arrangement of the room; individual student cards for requesting teacher assistance; procedures for changing from one activity to another; and the specification of roles for aides, students, and others in the daily operation of the classroom—were all instituted simultaneously at the beginning of the trial period. Procedures involving consequences for student behavior—systematic praise; awarding and exchanging of points; warnings for minor disruptive behavior; and self-correction procedures for students' written work—were added sequentially over a 1-month period.

In the pilot classroom, appropriate behavior during independent seatwork initially averaged less than 70% of the time; occasionally it went below 50%. After the procedures were in force, average appropriate behavior increased to above 90% during reading and arithmetic periods. When the procedures were temporarily stopped, average student appropriate behavior again fell below 70%. Reinstatement brought a return to levels exceeding 90% during reading and 80% during arithmetic periods.

Student and teacher responses also supported the use of the procedures. Students reported that they liked the more structured way their classroom operated. The teacher mentioned having to increase the amount of assigned work *four* times in the early weeks of the trial period as students learned how to use their time more efficiently and began to complete their work on a regular basis. Many of the teacher's colleagues—from other teachers to the assistant superintendent—came in to observe the class after the program began and praised the teacher for turning a group of "hard-to-teach" students into a group of good workers. The teacher also reported feeling much more confident about handling a variety of classroom management challenges. Since the pilot project, the teacher has trained more than two dozen other teachers in the same procedures.

Initial Development of the Procedures

The development of these procedures took place in two stages: (1) available literature in the area of classroom management was reviewed thoroughly, and (2) questions unanswered by the literature but of particular interest to us were addressed through our own research. This research included input obtained from students and teachers through the use of interviews and questionnaires.

Reviewing the Available Literature

We examined eight professional journals containing the majority of information published to date on classroom management for material on each topic of interest. Journal titles and issues reviewed are as follows:

Behavior Modification	Vol. 1, 1977 - Vol. 4, 1980
Behaviour Research and Therapy	Vol. 1, 1963 - Vol. 18, 1980
Behavior Therapy	Vol. 1, 1970 - Vol. 11, 1980
Education and Treatment of Children	Vol. 1, 1978 - Vol. 3, 1980
Journal of Applied Behavior Analysis	Vol. 1, 1968 - Vol. 13, 1980
Journal of Behavior Therapy and Experimental Psychiatry	Vol. 1, 1970 - Vol. 11, 1980
The Journal of School Psychology	Vol. 10, 1972 - Vol. 18, 1980
Psychology in the Schools	Vol. 7, 1970 - Vol. 17, 1980

Initially, we scanned tables of contents and indices of the journals to identify those classroom management topics on which several research studies had been conducted. Ten topics were identified, and they became the chapter headings for our manual of procedures.

Subsequently, the studies identified under each topic were reviewed in depth to determine (1) whether a consensus existed across various studies carried out on a given procedure; or (2) where no consensus existed, whether there was sufficient information in the area to generate specific questions we could research or whether the procedures, as used to date, contained some feature that could be recommended on the basis of logic, if not research. Where we found a consensus, we recommended the corresponding procedures. Where we found none, we presented the subsequent research findings of our staff or the logical features of procedures.

Conducting Research

In cases where no consensus regarding a classroom management procedure existed but a research direction was indicated by past work or by our own interests, we posed practical research questions and set out to answer these questions. Both experimental and questionnaire/interview approaches were used.

The experimental questions included these: (1) Can teachers who use a small-group instructional format teach a lesson and at the same time manage the behavior of students doing seatwork? (2) Can intermediate grade students be motivated to work harder or more carefully by being provided with game-like academic activities for doing so? (3) Are individualized work-completion criteria more beneficial for low-performing students than a single criterion for all students?

Teachers and students contributed to the procedure development through questionnaires and interviews. Teachers recognized as being particularly skilled were asked to describe the management strategies they used for a number of classroom situations. Both teachers and students listed their favorite and/or most innovative reinforcers, and some were rated by students for desirability (see Appendix B). Those students involved in the initial trial period reported whether or not they preferred the procedures from the program as compared to the procedures previously used.

Philosophy Behind the Procedures

The procedures presented in this program were developed within the context of the Direct Instruction Model for Follow Through, a successful approach created at the University of Oregon to provide compensatory education to disadvantaged students in the primary grades (K-3). These procedures have also been successfully used in regular and special education and with students in the intermediate grades.

Educationally disadvantaged students are those who come from low-income backgrounds and have had few opportunities for success in school. These students often have the potential to succeed in school, but they must be taught *very* efficiently. The Direct Instruction Model describes ways to teach these children so they can succeed.

The criterion for success in school is usually the ability to perform at or above an average level in both academics and deportment. In general, this level is set by nondisadvantaged students, who often have had more educational opportunities in their environment. Thus, when nothing is done in school to deal with the differences in children's backgrounds or characteristics relevant to school performance, the nondisadvantaged children often do better than the disadvantaged children both academically and behaviorally. This gap often widens as the children continue through school.

Is it simply an unavoidable fact of education that some students will do well, others will do poorly, and all the teacher can do is teach to the average students? The answer is a clear and definite *No*. It is *not* necessary for some children to do poorly. Many schools have developed programs that give low-performing students a better chance for success. Then why are traditional education programs so difficult for many disadvantaged and other low-performing students to master? In general, it is because this type of education is not sufficiently *structured* to allow these students to succeed. Yet traditional education can be restructured—or made more highly structured—for high-risk students so that they *can* do well in school.

Traditional Programs versus the Direct Instruction Model

The Direct Instruction Model for Follow Through is one example of a program that is structured to allow all students to succeed. It represents an entire educational philosophy—one that helps ensure students' success by using positive, structured, and responsive teaching and management procedures. The Model has been used most widely in the National Follow Through Program sponsored by the U.S. Office of Education. However, it also has been implemented successfully in other compensatory programs such as Title I, in special education programs, and in regular school programs.

The Direct Instruction philosophy is built on three major premises:

1. All children can be taught, and their behavior can be managed.

2. Children's learning failures must be seen as teaching failures, not as an inability of the child to learn. Similarly, their failure to behave appropriately must be seen as a failure to structure their environment sufficiently for successful conduct.

3. Low-performing children need to be taught at a faster-than-average rate, not at the same or a slower rate than other children; likewise, programs designed to teach them need to be more highly structured, not less.

The essential components of the Direct Instruction Model address six characteristics of traditional programs that seem to cause problems in teaching high-risk learners. Both the components and the characteristics are outlined in Table 1.1.

Table 1.1
**Comparison of Traditional Programs and
the Direct Instruction Model**

Problem Characteristics of Traditional Programs	Direct Instruction Model Components
Too much emphasis on nonacademic activities	Focus on *academic* objectives
Too much waste of available teaching time	*Structure* the use of time
Insufficient use of available classroom helpers	*Increase the number of helpers in the classroom,* giving them clearly defined responsibility, authority, and accountability
Inefficient teaching/management procedures	Use *efficient* teaching/management strategies
Inconsistent effort across time, tasks, and students	Use *standardized* teaching/management procedures (e.g., scripted presentation of management procedures)

Problem Characteristics of Traditional Programs	Direct Instruction Model Components
Insufficient information on student progress	*Frequently monitor* student progress, providing feedback to the teacher and student

Too much emphasis on nonacademic activities. Nonacademic activities include art, music, physical education, recess and lunch breaks, assemblies, and field trips. While any one of these activities may not require an excessive amount of time, when combined they consume a large portion of the time children spend in school. As a result, these activities must be put in perspective, and occasionally sacrificed, to ensure that sufficient time is available for teaching and practicing basic skills. The primary goal of schools is the achievement of basic skills by all students; if students fail to master these skills in the elementary grades, it is unlikely they will ever become proficient in their use.

In a program structured for success, the focus is clearly on academic objectives. While there may be little time for nonacademic pursuits other than those required by state standards, this does not mean that learning must be drudgery. Fun activities with academic objectives can be included to ensure that learning is enjoyable.

Too much waste of available teaching time. Few teachers deliberately slight academic needs when scheduling their school day. But many simply fail to realize how much time low-performing students need to master basic skills. The required amount of time can be provided by meeting three criteria: (1) sufficient scheduled time for academic instruction and practice, (2) adherence to the schedule, and (3) a high level of student on-task behavior. To reach these criteria, a teacher must become skilled at managing student behavior and orchestrating many different classroom events simultaneously.

In a program structured for success, blocks of time *believed* to be sufficient for academic instruction and practice are scheduled throughout the day. If the time allocated turns out to be insufficient—that is, if the students do not demonstrate a clear understanding of the lesson's objectives—the teacher can take advantage of "reserve" instructional or practice time later in the day or week. This time might occasionally be a period originally scheduled for a nonacademic activity, but responsiveness to students' academic needs is essential to keep students from falling behind.

In such a program, teachers also adhere to carefully planned schedules they have set. This does not mean that they always provide the activity listed on the schedule; rather, it means that they always start *academic* activities on time. Nonacademic activities may be postponed briefly if an academic period needs to run slightly overtime, or started early if all students master a lesson in *less* time than the teacher has allocated. Adherence to stopping and starting times also applies when one academic period follows another. If more time is needed for the first lesson, it must be inserted later in the day.

Students should be on-task most of the time in order to gain the maximum benefit from instruction. Usually this on-task level is set at about 80%, but higher levels (85 to 90%) are possible and were achieved consistently when the procedures described in this book were used. Teachers need to be aware of their students' level of involvement at any given time and be ready to alter classroom management strategies quickly in order to raise or maintain that involvement.

Insufficient use of available classroom helpers. Opportunities to give students extra teaching and practice sessions depend on available time and personnel. Often too much of the teacher's time is taken up by interruptions, paperwork (passing out and collecting papers, scoring them), and other "housekeeping" tasks (taking lunch and milk counts, erasing blackboards, organizing bulletin boards). None of these activities by itself requires much time on any one occasion, but over the course of a day or week each can detract considerably from available teaching time. In addition, potential helpers or instructors (aides, parents, peer tutors) may not be used often enough or may be used ineffectively.

A program geared to help students succeed makes use of all available helpers to provide more teaching and practice time. These people are most effective in the classroom when their efforts are coordinated and structured by the teacher. Many students are willing and eager to perform some of the "housekeeping" tasks typically done by teachers, freeing the teacher to do extra teaching or tutoring. Teachers' aides, volunteers, and peer tutors also can supply tutoring and practice time when properly instructed.

Inefficient teaching/management procedures. All teaching formats have some drawbacks that, if not compensated for, will interfere with learning. Large-group teaching sometimes holds back the quicker students while overwhelming slower ones. Yet individualized instruction offers little opportunity for teaching assistance if the student becomes confused. Even in small groups, slower students may stop participating as quicker students respond first. Also, the teacher may fail to check all students to correct their errors and make sure they have reached criterion.

In success-oriented programs the teacher (1) often teaches in a small-group instructional format; (2) keeps up a rapid pace during instruction to maintain all students' involvement in the lesson; (3) uses procedures to ensure that all students receive a maximum number of learning opportunities each lesson without being preempted by faster students; (4) corrects student errors immediately and brings students up to criterion on missed items; and (5) maintains student performance at high levels by reinforcing behaviors associated with success.

Inconsistent effort across time, tasks, and students. All teachers occasionally adopt resolutions to improve their efforts, take a deep breath and vow to do better, or make a fresh start by recommitting themselves to their jobs. However, it is difficult to maintain a constant effort without specific guidelines.

Programs structured for student success ensure consistency of effort by using standardized teaching and management procedures. In the Direct Instruction Model, for example, such procedures include scripted lessons and routinized teacher presentation techniques. Both have been evaluated extensively and found to be effective when used as described by the developers. The standardized classroom management procedures offered in this book also can help teachers systematically improve their classrooms.

Insufficient information on student progress. Traditionally, teachers determine and report on student progress every 6 or 9 weeks. As a result, a student having difficulty may not receive help for several days or even weeks. By that time the student may have fallen irrevocably behind in one or more academic areas.

Success-oriented programs continuously evaluate student progress. These programs include procedures for frequent monitoring using a variety of measures to provide feedback to the teacher. If students are not making adequate progress, the teacher can take immediate steps to help them catch up. This feedback loop is essential to the success of any educational program for low-performing students.

The Direct Instruction Model components are designed to create a classroom that ensures maximum learning through efficient use of time and personnel. These same components were drawn upon to assemble the classroom management procedures described in this text. Although the original purpose of the Model was to aid disadvantaged students, the procedures can benefit any classroom by increasing the amount of time spent on academic work and decreasing the time spent on unnecessary tasks or behavior problems.

Overview of the Procedures

This book contains procedures for dealing with every aspect of initially organizing a classroom and managing it on a day-to-day basis. It includes (1) organizing classroom space; (2) using volunteers and aides in the classroom; (3) using your attention to manage student behavior; (4) establishing and teaching classroom rules; (5) structuring and managing classroom time; (6) managing the flow of materials in the classroom; (7) handling student requests for assistance; (8) correcting student's work and keeping track of their performance; (9) dealing with minor behavior problems; (10) developing good work habits through a feedback chart; and (11) phasing out special procedures.

All these procedures are based on research done by others and published in the professional literature, research that our staff has done in the process of developing the procedures, or common logic, as validated by the judgments of several highly experienced classroom teachers who acted as consultants on this project. Thus, all together, the procedures form a data-based system for organizing and managing elementary school classrooms. This in turn means that if you use the procedures as described in the book, they should work for you as well.

The procedures can be used either in part or as a whole. If only a few areas of classroom management are a problem for you, you may need to use only the procedures designed for them. You should see improvement in those particular problems, but do not expect additional improvement in areas where procedures are not used.

On the other hand, if you would like to revamp your classroom procedures, or start a school year or a new term by structuring your classroom for success, or if you are a new teacher just starting out in the profession, we recommend that you implement all of the procedures. The extra effort required at the beginning will pay off for you in a short time as your students come to take school seriously, learn what your expectations are for them, and discover what they need to do to be successful in school.

The full program of procedures as presented here can be divided roughly into three parts. First are the *preparations* that must be made and the *background information* you will need before starting the program, which are presented in Chapters 2, 3, and 4. Second are *the procedures* to be instituted at the start of the program; these are found in Chapters 5 through 11. While the number of different procedures may make starting the program seem difficult, the program will become more manageable as the procedures become routine. Third, after several months of using the full program, some of the more specialized procedures can be *phased out*. Instructions for gradually eliminating these procedures are given in Chapter 12.

How the Procedures Differ from
Previous Classroom Management Approaches

Much work has been done in the past 15 years in the area of classroom management. However, the direction taken here differs from previous work in several ways.

Preventive Approach

Many of the classroom management approaches put forward to date have been reactive; that is, their procedures are applied only after the problem behavior has occurred. With such approaches, the teacher waits for problems to arise and then reacts to them. The underlying assumption is largely that students should behave well voluntarily and should not need to be motivated by the teacher.

Preventive approaches to classroom management, such as ours, assume that children react to the circumstances existing in the classroom at any given time. Thus, instead of waiting for behavior problems to occur, the teacher can prevent them by providing circumstances that motivate students to behave appropriately. This can be done by using a variety of antecedent events (events that set the occasion for student behavior, such as making rules, scheduling, and arranging classroom layout) and positive consequences (things the students will work to earn, such as praise, points, and activity rewards).

Whole-Class Approach

Traditionally, classroom management procedures have focused on the behavior of individual students—usually those students causing most of the disruptions in the classroom. This feature is closely related to the reactive nature of early behavior management efforts in the classroom.

Here we take a whole-class approach rather than an individual student focus. This doesn't mean we overlook the individual differences and needs of various students. However, a truly preventive approach has to look at the whole class in order to consider all possible sources of problems. This program attempts to structure for success by taking into account all students and all classroom routines that are part of a normal school day.

Multi-Grade Approach

This book synthesizes much of the classroom management research done to date, including the research we did ourselves, and makes specific management recommendations for use in elementary school classrooms. The procedures presented here address both primary grade needs, such as learning the rules and procedures of the classroom, and intermediate grade needs, such as working independently for extended periods of time without disrupting others, completing work on time at a high level of accuracy, and managing one's time.

Developmental differences between upper elementary students and lower grade students (those at the preschool, kindergarten, first and second grade levels) need to be considered in any classroom management approach. For example, the younger students generally respond well to enthusiastic teacher praise. Older students might work better for more subtle teacher praise, for peer recognition, or when competing in teams with another group of students. Also, more written work usually is required at the upper grade levels, with less teacher-directed time in the school day and more need to manage students' seatwork behavior. For these reasons, you will want to apply these classroom management procedures differently at the intermediate grade levels than you will in the primary grades.

Integrative Approach

Previous work done to manage student behavior in the classroom has been fragmentary. Typically, it has addressed student behaviors one at a time, while ignoring entire groups of skills that might be more important. While each type of student response has a significant impact on the classroom, teachers cannot be expected to scour the research literature and assemble techniques to deal with each behavior separately. Instead, those who develop programs must synthesize the work done to date into a unified, cohesive body of information containing procedures teachers can use for all aspects of classroom management. We have attempted to do this in our book.

Comprehensive Approach

Students' behavior can be analyzed for classroom management by using an "ABCD" scheme. "B," the *behavior*, is preceded by *antecedent events*, or "A." Antecedent events are those factors existing in the environment prior to a behavior that make that behavior more or less likely to occur. Putting a new toy on a shelf within easy reach may be an antecedent for undesirable behavior; separating two talkative friends in the classroom may be an antecedent for good behavior. The third letter, "C," represents the *consequences* to the student for performing a behavior. A fourth element to consider is "D," or *data* on the frequency or duration of a behavior.

Traditional classroom management has focused almost exclusively on "C," the management of consequences following student behavior. But the management of antecedent events and the use of data to monitor students' performance in the classroom often have been overlooked.

The control of antecedent events and the use of student data are integral parts of the program presented here. They are used in addition to some simple procedures recommended for controlling consequences. This combination is more comprehensive and thus more likely to be effective.

Standardized Approach

Classroom management strategies are sometimes stated so theoretically they are of little practical use in the classroom; in reality, the details of applying a technique can be as important as selecting the technique itself. A strategy that is promising in theory may fail because it is applied incorrectly.

The solution to this problem is to present any strategy in detail. If a procedure has been developed, evaluated, and found to work in a given form, it should be recommended to others *in that form* or its effectiveness may be reduced. By providing careful instructions for each of the procedures recommended in this book, we have increased your chances of success.

Learning the Procedures

Each of the following chapters describes a group of procedures used to manage one aspect of classroom routine. The chapter usually begins with a definition of unfamiliar terms followed by an explanation of why this particular topic is being addressed under the heading (*Why . . .*). If others besides the teacher can help with the procedures, they are mentioned (*Who . . .*). The bulk of each chapter is concerned with how the procedures are to be established and maintained (*How to . . .*). Most topics end with an "Implementation Checklist" you can use to determine whether you have done everything required to implement the procedures correctly (there will sometimes be more than one topic to a chapter).

At the end of each chapter "A Survey of Research" provides a brief review of literature relevant to the chapter topic(s). This section is followed by a reference list for the works cited in the chapter.

Many chapters will have one or more "scripts" to use with students. Introductory scripts are designed to introduce new procedures and to ensure that all students understand what behavior you expect of them. Review scripts are used as reminders for your students after the initial introduction and following any break in school routine. You will not have to memorize these scripts word for word, but you should review and practice them so your presentation is close to the original phrasing and content. Do not read them from the book; you will be less spontaneous and less able to observe your students' responses. The best presentation will be one done enthusiastically in your own style. It should be paced briskly, not by talking quickly, but by minimizing pauses between questions.

In each script, you carefully explain to students the rules for a particular procedure. You state the rule itself in a simple sentence, which the entire class then repeats. Responding in unison gives students many opportunities to participate during a lesson and thus increase their learning. When done correctly, this technique also prevents the slow responders from relying on the fast responders for answers, rather than thinking for themselves.

The students' response should occur only after your signal. You can use any signal that is audible or visible to all students, such as tapping a pencil, clapping your hands, or holding your hand out as if stopping traffic, then dropping it to your side. When you ask for a response, you should pause 1 second before signaling. This pause will allow everyone to get ready to respond. Praise them for answering on signal. If some students come in too early or too late for a signal, say "Wait for my signal" (if too soon) or "Answer as soon as I signal" (if delayed). All students should respond before you continue, as this ensures their attention and participation in the activity. If one or more students do not answer, say "I have to hear everybody" and look at those who are not participating. Then try again. Best results have been obtained when all children have been required to participate.

Occasionally the script will direct you to call on individual students for responses. Be sure to call on a different individual each time.

Finally, these scripts are meant to help your students understand your expectations for their behavior, not to teach them the exact wording of the rules. As a result, don't waste too much time trying to get students to memorize the rule statements. They will learn what to do if you praise them for following the rules and hold them to high standards of behavior.

Please read all the chapters before beginning your program. You may find you want to use only selected portions, or you may choose to do the entire program but need to plan how and when to introduce each set of procedures. After you have reviewed the entire program, you will see all of the possible benefits and the amount of effort needed to achieve them. We do believe that by following the procedures as we have described them here, you will see significant improvements in the classroom management areas you choose to work on.

A Survey of Research

Over the past 15 years, dozens of studies have addressed the question "What factors contribute to teacher effectiveness?" Despite varied procedural orientations, methodological approaches, and geographic locales, the results of these studies have been remarkably similar and mutually supportive. From this body of literature, we can begin for the first time to distill some empirically validated principles to guide future classroom organizational, management, and instructional efforts. Some of the findings might not seem particularly profound; they may have already occurred to you as common sense. But backed by supporting scientific data, they are all the more compelling. Other findings may be new to you. Put together, these findings provide an empirical base for building an entire classroom system designed for success.

The studies tell us several important facts. First of all, teachers' expectations *and* their tolerances contribute significantly to student levels of achievement and classroom behavior (Brophy & Evertson, 1976; Good & Brophy, 1978). Furthermore, the standards set by teachers seem to be self-fulfilling prophecies for students. When expectations are high and tolerances are low, students achieve at higher levels and exhibit fewer conduct problems. When these standards are reversed, so, too, is student performance. For example, Good and Brophy (1978) found that teachers tended to seat low-performing students further away from themselves, called on these students less, praised them fewer times, and criticized them more than they did average and high performers. These appear to be some of the teacher behaviors that translate into poor student performance.

Studies on how teachers affect students also describe the demands typically placed on a classroom teacher. Doyle (1980) found that such demands are multi-dimensional, simultaneous, and unpredictable. Given these conditions, Doyle asserts that the approach to classroom organization and management which is most likely to succeed is a preventive one, in which a majority of potential problems are anticipated and prepared for by a teacher who is organized, flexible, and able to handle multiple task demands.

Kounin (1977) studied effective teachers and found that they shared several characteristics that distinguished them from less effective colleagues. Successful classroom managers (1) dealt with several things at once; (2) judged quickly whether an event in the classroom was important or relatively unimportant; (3) exhibited an on-going awareness of all that was happening in the classroom despite numerous distractions; (4) timed their actions carefully for maximum effect (e.g., maintaining eye contact after giving a direction to facilitate compliance); (5) maintained group focus by giving attention to more than one student at a time—they did not get overly involved with a single student; and (6) managed movement within the classroom by controlling student transitions.

It also appears from the available literature that the effective teacher manages a classroom differently at different times of the year. Emmer, Evertson, and Anderson (1979) reported that at the beginning of the year, effective teachers (1) maximized contact with students; (2) monitored students frequently; (3) intervened quickly to deal with behavior problems; (4) ensured high levels of time on-task; (5) provided frequent and detailed feedback; (6) structured activities and materials carefully; (7) used task signaling systems; (8) established clear routines and expectations; and (9) rehearsed with students the behaviors that matched those expectations. By the time several weeks had passed, these teachers were able to reduce this structure greatly.

Developmental differences also are important considerations in managing classrooms. Brophy and Evertson (1976) stated that differences in students from early to late childhood call for different approaches to management. Children in kindergarten through second or third grade, for example, tend to respond best to direct instruction, small steps of progress, a rapid pace, overteaching of content, and teacher praise. Older students respond less to the authority of the teacher's position and more to the influence of their peers. These students tend to do well when challenged, when divided into teams for academic competition, and when peer influence works for the teacher's goals, rather than against them.

Various other articles support our approach to classroom management. Rosenshine (1976, 1979) and Berliner (1979) used the term "direct instruction" to refer to the set of teacher variables they found that were closely related to teacher effectiveness. These characteristics correspond on nearly a one-to-one basis with the components of the Direct Instruction Model, upon which the structured classroom model in this book is based. In another study, Corno (1979) made a case for the efficient use of time as a critical factor in students' and teachers' success in school. And Ward and Tikunoff (1979) discussed the valuable role non-teachers can play in the classroom management process.

References

Berliner, D. Tempus educare. In P. Peterson & H. Walberg (Eds.), *Research on teaching: Concepts, findings, and implications*. Berkeley: McCutchan, 1979.

Brophy, J., & Evertson, C. *Learning from teaching: A developmental perspective*. Boston: Allyn and Bacon, 1976.

Corno, L. Classroom instruction and the matter of time. In D. Duke (Ed.), *Classroom management: Seventy-eighth yearbook of the National Society for the Study of Education*. Chicago: University of Chicago Press, 1979.

Doyle, W. *Classroom management*. West Lafayette, Ind.: Kappa Delta Pi, 1980.

Emmer, E., Evertson, C., & Anderson, L. *Effective classroom management at the beginning of the school year*. Austin: Research and Development Center for Teacher Education, University of Texas, 1979.

Good, T., & Brophy, J. *Looking in classrooms* (2nd ed.). New York: Harper & Row, 1978.

Kounin, J. *Discipline and group management in classrooms*. Huntington, N.Y.: Krieger, 1977.

Rosenshine, B. Classroom instruction. In N. L. Gage (Ed.), *The psychology of teaching methods: Seventy-fifth yearbook of the National Society for the Study of Education.* Chicago: University of Chicago Press, 1976.

Rosenshine, B. Content, time, and direct instruction. In P. L. Peterson & H. J. Walberg (Eds.), *Research on teaching: Concepts, findings, and implications.* Berkeley: McCutchan, 1979.

Ward, B., & Tikunoff, W. Utilizing nonteachers in the instructional process. In D. Duke (Ed.), *Classroom management: Seventy-eighth yearbook of the National Society for the Study of Education.* Chicago: National Society for the Study of Education, 1979.

Chapter 2

Organizing Classroom Space

Organizing classroom space means arranging the furniture (student and teacher desks), room dividers, teaching and other specific activity areas, and wall space in the classroom to create an effective learning environment. In this section we discuss the purposes of organizing classroom space and provide specific procedures for accomplishing this task.

Why Use Special Considerations to Organize Classroom Space?

While teachers organize their classroom space in some manner, they may have trouble pinpointing why they do it a particular way and whether their organizational plan works. Yet how classroom space is organized can have a considerable effect on student behavior.

The teacher's primary goal is to set up an environment that will encourage students to do their best in school. The location of student desks, the teacher's desk, classroom partitions, and teaching and materials stations can play an important part not only in the efficient management of a classroom but also in how effectively students learn. Proper classroom arrangement also enables the teacher to carry out various teaching activities more efficiently. Since the classroom can have such an impact on teacher and students alike, some of the best teachers take great care in setting up their classrooms at the beginning of the school year. In this chapter, we will look at some of the factors they consider.

Classroom Organization and Student Behavior

Proper classroom arrangement can affect student behavior in four important areas. Each of these areas can be managed to improve student performance.

First, carefully arranging the classroom can decrease student noise and disruption. For example, students who are seated at separate desks are less likely to talk and more likely to work and pay attention. Student disruption is one of the major reasons many children do not perform at their level of capability. When teachers cut down on noise and disruptive behavior in their classrooms, student achievement levels often increase. In addition, the teachers' and students' time can be spent on academic activities. This factor is especially important for students who are below grade level; the more time they spend on subject areas, the greater the opportunity for them to catch up.

Second, proper organization of classroom space can improve the level and quality of student interactions. Because students spend a great deal of time interacting with each other, a teacher must pay close attention to the quality of these exchanges. Using effective classroom organization, teachers can eliminate many inappropriate student exchanges such as excessive talking, moving around the classroom, or teasing other students. This fact is especially true of students who are below their grade level. Characteristically, these students spend much of their school time involved with other students when they should be working on their academic activities. Teachers often report that while many students do well in organized instructional activities, they have problems working independently. By properly organizing classroom space, teachers can decrease the amount of inappropriate student exchanges and help students work harder during their independent study periods.

Third, effective classroom arrangements can increase *desirable* student interaction. Quiet places, pillows, books, pictures, chairs, games, and a variety of materials can help teach different kinds of social interactions. Materials that require cooperative efforts will teach cooperation; materials that require problem solving will teach creativity, and so on. Part of each school day can be focused on teaching sharing, conflict negotiation, cooperation, compromise, self-evaluation, communication, and friendship. Open areas will encourage students to move from one activity to another. Also, students are more likely to use materials that are readily available to them.

Efficient use of available classroom space can also be achieved with proper organization of the classroom environment. Many teachers find that arranging work stations, free-time areas, and independent work space is an effective learning aid. For example, planned arrangement of chalkboards, bookcases, and materials will increase the efficiency of instructional and transitional periods. Also, teachers find it important to place the direct instruction areas where they can easily observe student activities in other work stations. Such positioning helps them manage all the activities occurring in the classroom at one time.

Last, the proper organization of classroom space can increase the percentage of time that students spend on their academic tasks. This effect is particularly important to students who are behind academically, since they must work harder if they are to catch up to their classmates.

Classroom Organization and Teacher Performance

Besides the effects on student learning, proper arrangement of classroom space also has an impact on teacher performance. Such activities as rate of praise, student corrections, and supervision are all affected by the physical arrangement of the classroom. Teachers must see positive activity in order to encourage it. A room that allows broad visibility will enable teachers to monitor many children and activities at one time. Each of these teacher behaviors is related to increased academic performance. Therefore, if the learning environment can be arranged to help teachers develop these behaviors, it will also assist them in the difficult task of improving student performance. In addition, organization of classroom space accommodates other classroom management procedures described in this book, such as posting the classroom rules and point chart; circulating among students to praise them, correct their work, and assist them; and passing out and collecting papers.

How to Organize Classroom Space

The physical arrangement of a classroom as described in this chapter is illustrated in Figure 2.1. The basic plan includes eight components.

Figure 2.1
Physical Arrangement of the Classroom

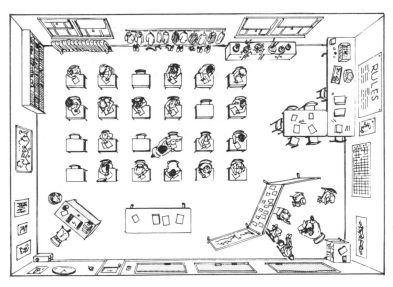

1. *Student desks.* Student desks should be separated, in rows, and should face toward the chalkboard and away from the windows. This

arrangement will help minimize disruptions and unwanted interactions during those times when you want students to work independently. You also will be able to move around the room easily to praise students, help them when they need it, and correct their work as you go. Place low-performing students, or students with behavior problems, in the front row. They will be easier to monitor, and you might be able to draw them into more learning activities. However, avoid seating them next to other disruptive students. If they are near higher performing or well-behaved students, they may be influenced by these positive models and improve more rapidly.

2. *Teacher's desk.* Place the teacher's desk in one of the front corners of the room facing the students. If there is an aide in the room, place the aide's desk in the back on the opposite side of the room from the teacher's desk. These arrangements will provide the best opportunities to monitor students when they are at their desks. However, you may find that you spend a great deal of time teaching a small group. Thus, if the room seems overly crowded with student desks, teaching stations, a self-correction station, and so on, you might consider removing the teacher's and/or aide's desks. One teacher did so after discovering that she spent most of her time teaching lessons, circulating among students, and supervising other activities, and never used her desk. We are not necessarily recommending that you take this step; it is simply an option for you to consider.

3. *Classroom partitions.* If possible, use movable partitions such as lightweight screens, chalkboards, bulletin boards, storage shelves/cabinets, or coatracks on wheels. These will give you the maximum flexibility for classroom structure and allow you to change the structure as needed during the day or week. If another adult is in the classroom, you might want to screen off a small-group instructional activity from the rest of the class to minimize distractions. If you are alone in the room, you will want to remove the partition so that you can monitor the behavior of other students in the room while you teach.

4. *Teaching stations.* Arrange teaching stations in any corner of the room not occupied by teacher or aide desks. To reduce distractions, have the student chairs face the wall. However, the teacher's chair should face the room so that you can monitor seatworkers' behavior while you teach.

5. *Self-correction station.* Arrange a student self-correction station against part of one wall by placing a table and a few chairs there or by using a counter.

6. *Materials station.* Put a medium- to large-sized table in the center of the front of the room as a place for materials that are being passed out or collected.

7. *Activity stations.* Student activity stations can be set up in various parts of the room. They can offer materials, ideas, and projects that encourage additional practice of academic, social, motor, or creativity skills.

8. *Bulletin boards.* Part of your bulletin board space can be used for traditional artistic or seasonal displays, but some of it should be reserved to post materials described later in this book. Classroom rules and schedules, a feedback chart and any related graphs, and other materials pertaining to the program should be posted prominently.

If you want students to act differently during various parts of the day, or on different days, then rearrange the space on those days. For example, it may be appropriate at times for students to share and talk quietly and work together such as when doing an art project. You will then need to teach students *how* to share and talk quietly, even when their desks are touching.

A Survey of Research

Although research literature presently contains little detailed advice on designing elementary school classrooms, recommendations can be gleaned from work done in related areas. However, because the number of studies done in this area is small, these findings should be considered suggestive rather than conclusive.

Twardosz, Cataldo, and Risley (1974) examined the comparative effects of open and partitioned day-care/preschool environments. In the open conditions, partitions that separated various activity areas were removed. The series of experiments demonstrated that an open environment (1) substantially increased the amount of time a child was visible to a supervising adult; (2) was as conducive to small-group, pre-academic activities as was a separate room; and (3) greatly reduced the effort required to supervise staff. Since the power of teacher monitoring has been well documented, visibility of students and staff may be an important organizational variable. The importance of the physical environment for student behavior has also been addressed by the work of Hewett (1967, 1968), in which the design of the classroom environment is a primary variable.

The role of spacing between students has been addressed in three studies. Krantz and Risley (Note 1) experimentally demonstrated that spacing preschool disadvantaged children apart, rather than letting them crowd together during teaching demonstrations, increased their attention to the teacher. Prescott, Jones, and Kritchevsky (1967) found that as physical space decreased in a school setting (1) the teacher's manner was measured as less sensitive and less friendly; (2) the children were rated as less interested in activities and less involved in interactions; and (3) negative interactions among students increased. Axelrod, Hall, and Tams (1979) systematically varied student seating during independent work periods and found that more distance between the students (i.e., separated desks rather than table clusters) was related to increased levels of on-task behavior and decreased levels of disruptiveness.

Relationships between classroom design and student performance have also been reported by Weinstein (1979). Weinstein found that this relationship persisted even with high-performing students and rather small changes in the design of the physical environment (e.g., teacher position in the classroom). Through such changes, Weinstein was able to influence students' interaction with their materials, the amount of time students spent being distracted from their assigned tasks, and the level and intensity of teachers' questioning patterns.

Adams (1969) and Adams and Biddle (1970) reported a finding that parallels that of Weinstein. They learned that a student's seating position can greatly affect the amount of interaction the student has with the teacher during classroom discussions. They reported that most of the teacher's interaction was with students who were seated in the center front portion of the class or in a line from the center front students to the back of the room. That is, students who were seated to either side of center were not as actively engaged by the teacher. To the extent that this variable eventually relates to student achievement, seating position can have an effect on student performance in school. Teachers' circulation among students during class activities might help counter this tendency and distribute attention more evenly.

In a final, related study, Rist (1970) found that teachers assigned seating locations to students on variables other than the need for frequent monitoring or greater interaction. Rist found that a teacher in an inner-city kindergarten class assigned students their seats on the basis of subjectively interpreted social criteria. For example, students who displayed middle-class attitudes and behavior (as determined by the teacher) were placed nearest the teacher. Those seen as deviating from this "ideal" were seated farther away. Teachers need to be aware of these tendencies and determine seating assignments and interaction patterns based on the students' need for the teacher's attention or supervision, not on factors of convenience or social desirability.

Reference Notes

1. Krantz, P. J., & Risley, T. R. The organization of group care environments: Behavioral ecology in the classroom. Paper presented at the meeting of the American Psychological Association, Honolulu, September 1972.

References

Adams, R. S. Location as a feature of instructional interaction. *Merrill Palmer Quarterly*, 1969, *15*, 309-322.

Adams, R. S., & Biddle, B. J. *Realities of teaching: Explorations with video tape.* New York: Holt, Rinehart & Winston, 1970.

Axelrod, S., Hall, R. V., & Tams, A. Comparison of two common classroom seating arrangements. *Academic Therapy*, 1979, *15*, 29-36.

Hewett, F. M. Educational engineering with emotionally disturbed children. *Exceptional Children*, 1967, *33*, 459-467.

Hewett, F. M. *The emotionally disturbed child in the classroom: A developmental strategy for educating children with maladaptive behavior.* Boston: Allyn and Bacon, 1968.

Prescott, E., Jones, E., & Kritchevsky, S. *Group day care as a child rearing environment: An observational study of day care programs.* Pasadena, Calif.: Pacific Lakes College, 1967. (ERIC Document Reproduction Service No. ED 024 453)

Rist, R. C. Student social class and teacher expectations: The self-fulfilling prophecy in ghetto education. *Harvard Educational Review*, 1970, *40*, 411-451.

Twardosz, S., Cataldo, M. F., & Risley, T. R. Open environment design for infant and toddler day care. *Journal of Applied Behavior Analysis*, 1974, *7*, 529-546.

Weinstein, C. S. The physical environment of the school. *Review of Educational Research*, 1979, *49*, 577-610.

Chapter 3

Developing Roles for Others in the Classroom Management Process

Helping all students learn as much as possible is a difficult job that can be done more efficiently if you arrange for classroom support from other people. In this chapter, we discuss why and how to get help for your classroom and how to make the involvement of others work for you.

Why Involve Others in the Classroom?

Using additional people to assist you in the classroom will enable students who need extra instruction, practice, or encouragement to receive additional, personalized attention. This procedure also helps students learn to work with a variety of adults and allows you to run a smooth and efficient classroom that maximizes learning opportunities for *all* of your students.

Who Can Participate?

Before you begin using the procedures, the teachers who taught your students last year can give you useful information about the children. Once you begin using the procedures, classroom helpers may include parents, volunteers from the community, aides, classmates, older students, principals, counselors, consultants, and other people in the school who are willing to help your students learn. Don't overlook any possibilities for acquiring skilled volunteer help.

How to Involve Others
in the Classroom Management Process

There are five steps in the process of acquiring assistance in your classroom from others.

Talk to Your Students' Previous Teachers

When you begin planning your classroom at the start of the new year, set aside some time to talk with the teachers who taught your students previously. These teachers have had an entire academic year to get acquainted with your students. They can point out who may need extra help or what techniques were particularly motivating for students—information that can be valuable to you as you plan the coming year's program. You can save considerable time by starting the school term with positive, specific data about your students.

To get the maximum benefits from these meetings, we recommend following three basic guidelines.

1. *Don't allow the conversation to become a gossip session.* Have specific questions you want to ask; write them down if necessary to help you structure the conversation. By doing so, you will ensure that the time you spend will yield valuable information. We have found that questions such as the following are an efficient way to elicit information:

- How far did the students get in last year's curriculum?
- What level of mastery did they attain?
- How much help and monitoring do they need in seatwork?
- What kinds of incentives are effective in motivating the students?

2. *Try to concentrate on the positive.* Talk about student performance does not always have to focus on the negative. Ask for the positive attributes, both social and academic, of individual students. An understanding of students' academic strengths can be helpful when you attempt to identify areas in which students can work independently. Such advance information can help eliminate the behavior problems that result when students are asked to work by themselves on material too hard or too easy for them.

After speaking with the students' previous teachers, develop a list of positive constructive information about your students, noting in particular student strengths that could be used as a resource for your classroom. For example, if you know that a student is coming to you with strong skills in math, that student might be a good math tutor for someone else. Students who are responsible and good at detailed work might like to help with classroom record-keeping or materials preparation.

3. *Get specific information about students' previous academic performance.* Concentrate on such details as the following:

- Which subjects does the student like and dislike?
- How much practice does it take for the student to learn new material (on the average)?
- What preskills does the student have in the major academic areas?

Knowing this information will make it easier to preplan your classroom organization.

Develop Ways Others Can Help You Maximize Student Learning

Assistants can be helpful in many ways. Aides, parents, community volunteers, classmates, or older peers may:

- Listen to students read;
- Drill basic math facts;
- Praise independent seatwork;
- Help children correct their own papers;
- Drill children on difficult reading words;
- Direct small-group activities;
- Develop and supervise art, music, cooking, or sewing projects.

Principals, consultants, janitors, cooks, bus drivers, or secretaries may:

- Send "good day" notes home;
- Make positive phone calls to parents;
- Listen to children read;
- Watch students who are working hard;
- Teach students something unique: a fact, a foreign language phrase, some sign language, a gymnastic stunt, a magic trick, or a joke;
- Engage students in conversation;
- Praise students;
- Let students help with the secretarial, janitorial, cooking, and other duties.

These lists are merely possibilities. Be creative. Brainstorm. Ask students and others for ideas. You may identify many ways throughout the year in which people can be helpful.

Then determine which tasks are best accomplished by which assistants. Some guidelines for matching tasks with people may be helpful. First, ask yourself the following questions:

- Which jobs are the most complicated, difficult, or important?
- Which jobs must be done most frequently and reliably?
- Which jobs require good reading, math, or spelling skills?
- Which jobs require good organization and neatness?
- Which jobs require good affective skills (listening, smiling, communicating, empathizing, supporting)?
- Which jobs require people with special state certification or insurance liability?

Develop a list of job tasks and requirements from these questions.

Second, determine the following:

- Which students demonstrate learning or behavior problems?
- Which students would benefit from more contact with peers, adults, men, women, authority figures, older people, or experts?

Once job tasks are developed and student problems and preferences determined, match assistants to students by watching the assistants work and observing their strengths and weaknesses.

Recruit people to help in your classroom on a regular basis. Volunteers may be found through parents of students, through other teachers who have used volunteers in the past, or through the local high schools, colleges, or universities. Local community groups like Parent-Teacher Associations, religious groups, Girl Scouts and Boy Scouts, senior citizen activity groups, clubs and lodges, and volunteer councils might help identify volunteers for you. Recruiting can include word-of-mouth information; newsletters; posted notices; radio, TV, and newspaper announcements; or public announcements at community and school meetings. Seek out people who are reliable and motivated—people your students will find interesting, exciting, consistent, and kind. Some people will be willing to work many hours each week; others will agree to come only infrequently. Sign them all up (Figure 3.1 is an example of a volunteer sign-up sheet). Keep looking: good help is worth a thorough search.

Teach assistants exactly what to do: when, where, what, who, how. For help to be truly helpful, it must be an organized, positive effort on everyone's part. People new to your classroom are often uncertain about what to do with children and may be confused by the complexities of daily classroom routine. They will need close supervision and careful instruction at the beginning.

Train volunteers *before* they work with the children. Let them spend a day simply observing, followed by some time with you to ask questions. Then set up a time when there are no children present so that you can show them exactly what you want them to do. Be specific about such items as:

- Where they get the materials;
- Where the materials belong when the lesson is over;
- Where they work with the children;
- Which children they work with on which days;
- Where the activity should occur;
- What the classroom rules are;
- When they should get help from you;
- Exactly what the instruction should look like;
- How long the activity should last;
- How to deal with potential problems.

Make up a chart, such as the one shown in Figure 3.2, to record exactly when volunteers are expected to be present and what they are supposed

Figure 3.1
List of Volunteers

Name	Phone Number	Days Volunteering	Classroom Jobs

Figure 3.2
Volunteer Schedule

Volunteer _____

Day	Time	Activity	Materials	Location	Students	Rules

to do. Post the chart where you and your assistants can see it easily. Any changes in the volunteer schedule can be noted on the chart.

Successful training usually includes (1) demonstrating the activity, (2) allowing practice time, and (3) providing constructive feedback. For a model procedure for tutoring, see the flash card system described by Silbert, Carnine, and Stein (1981). Initially, be available to give considerable support and constructive suggestions. Observe how the volunteers work. Remember to establish clear expectations and communicate them adequately to volunteers. You need to be direct, firm, positive, encouraging, and stimulating. Continue to provide support and feedback throughout the entire school year.

One method of providing feedback to beginning volunteers is to record their performance on a daily checklist (see Figure 3.3). You can mark activities the volunteer has done correctly each day, and discuss the checklist with the person at the end of each week for the first few weeks. Set goals for improvement during each meeting, and check the following week for progress. When you feel more confident about the volunteer's capabilities, the feedback reviews can be scheduled monthly; later they can be eliminated altogether.

Reward jobs well done. Let volunteers know they are valued. Teach students that the assistants are an important part of the classroom and have them acknowledge volunteers' efforts. Possible rewards you can provide your volunteers may include:

- Going out for breakfast, lunch, or coffee;
- Bringing donuts, fruit, etc., for snacks;
- Giving cards saying thanks—from you, the principal, or the students;
- Holding recognition ceremonies in the classroom, at a school assembly, or at a community gathering;
- Providing opportunities for increased responsibility;
- Publishing articles or pictures in school, community, or city newspapers;
- Providing opportunities to train others;
- Providing opportunities to make presentations to a school or community gathering.

Involving the Principal and/or Counselor in Positive Classroom Management

Two procedures can be used to involve the principal and/or counselor in classroom management in a positive, constructive way.

Figure 3.3
Checklist for Classroom Helpers

Name _____ Date _____

	Mon	Tue	Wed	Thu	Fri
1. Arrive on time					
2. Come in quietly					
3. Locate all needed materials					
4. Work in correct place					
5. Do the assigned activity					
6. Do the activity with the assigned students					
7. Do the activity the right way					
8. End at the right time					
9. Put all materials away					
10. Leave quietly					
11. Handle problems effectively					
12. Be encouraging, supportive to students					
13. Speak loud enough, soft enough					
14. Go fast enough, slow enough					
15. Enforce classroom rules					
16. Communicate clearly					
TOTAL					

Summary of strengths

Summary of weaknesses

Goal for next week

The Principal's Game

The first is called the Principal's Game. The objective is to have the principal (or counselor) and classroom teacher work together to manage a disruptive classroom. The teacher starts by telling the pupils they are not working as hard as they could, but there is a "game" that will help them work harder. The following game components are given:

- Teams are formed according to seating rows—one row equals one team.
- A bell (kitchen timer) will ring six times during the class; each time it rings, the teacher determines which teams are working hard and following classroom rules.
- If each member of the team is working, the entire team receives a point marked on the chalkboard. But if one member of a team is not working when the bell rings, the team does not receive a point.
- All teams could win, but to win, a team has to earn at least 5 points.

Later, the principal comes into the room and asks the winning teams to stand. The principal then acknowledges their performance and talks briefly with them about their work, what they are learning, and so on.

The result of this program can be a dramatic increase in appropriate classroom behavior. A previously disruptive classroom can be transformed into a roomful of hardworking, cooperative, and enthusiastic students, striving to earn the privilege of being recognized by the principal.

The Principal's Lottery

A second procedure, the Principal's Lottery, differs in two important aspects from the Principal's Game. In this game a daily lottery is held and pupils work for the privilege of having their names drawn at random. Parents of the lottery winners are phoned by the principal and informed of their child's exemplary behavior.

As in the Principal's Game, the teacher informs the pupils that they are not doing as well as they can. The teacher then describes the behavior expected from them and gives the details of the Principal's Lottery. The procedure consists of the following components:

- The teacher plays a prerecorded audio tape with six randomly spaced "beeps."
- Pupils who are following previously defined classroom rules when the "beep" sounds receive a mark by their name on the chalkboard.
- Any pupil who receives five or six marks in a day is eligible for the daily drawing.
- Two names are selected from among the eligible students.
- Parents are phoned by the principal and told about their child's good work.

■ Pupils who are selected on one day are not excluded from being selected again.

Both these games include the principal in the management of disruptive classrooms in a positive way. A school counselor could also play the role of reinforcement agent. The Principal's Game and the Principal's Lottery are efficient, requiring only 3 to 5 minutes of the principal's or counselor's time each day.

Programs such as the two just described can make pupils feel better about themselves and their principal, can help a teacher with a disruptive class situation, and can help the principal—who is sometimes seen by students only as a disciplinarian—be involved in more positive ways with the students in the school.

Involving Students in Peer-Tutoring

Students can help others and themselves to learn by tutoring schoolmates. Setting up a peer-tutoring program, and keeping it going, involves six major steps:

1. *Decide to do it.* Decide what purpose a peer-tutoring program will have in the classroom. How will it help? What needs will it meet? Why is it the best option?

2. *Determine roles for tutors.* Decide what role tutors will play. Will they provide instruction in academic skills, provide rewards for academic or social behavior, keep records, organize materials, or act as models?

3. *Determine the skills tutors will teach.* Will tutors teach academic, social, motor, play, or self-help skills? Will they teach reading, math, handwriting, shoe-tying, kickball, or coloring?

4. *Recruit and select tutors.* Decide who will be the tutors: high-performing peers, older students, or low-performing peers? Encourage students to be involved in the program, and select those who will be the most successful.

5. *Train the tutors.* Carefully teach tutors the skills they need to be successful. Take time to train them to observe, present materials, reinforce, and collect data, as necessary. Train them to work professionally.

6. *Supervise and reinforce.* Once the program has begun, continue to supervise and praise the tutors and their students.

A more detailed analysis of a tutoring program includes 14 comprehensive steps, which are itemized in the Peer-Tutoring Program Checklist.

Peer-Tutoring Program Checklist

_____ 1. Specify goals
  _____ for learners
  _____ for peers
_____ 2. Specify reasons for implementing program
_____ 3. Specify peer role
_____ 4. Specify practical constraints
  _____ learner
  _____ peer
  _____ procedural
  _____ setting
  _____ target skill
_____ 5. Develop monitoring system
  _____ who will monitor
  _____ procedure
  _____ schedule
  ___ materials needed
_____ 6. Develop management system
  _____ peer behavior
    _____ type of reinforcer
    _____ schedule
    _____ who delivers
    _____ type of response cost
    _____ schedule
    _____ who delivers
  _____ learner behavior
    _____ type of reinforcer
    _____ schedule
    _____ who delivers
    _____ type of response cost
    _____ schedule
    _____ who delivers
_____ 7. Develop and organize materials
_____ 8. Determine schedule and setting for tutoring
  _____ where interaction will occur
  _____ during what time of day interaction will occur
  _____ how long each interaction will last
_____ 9. Recruit volunteers
_____ 10. Select peer managers
  _____ develop job sample tasks
  _____ develop rating criteria
  _____ observe performance on job sample
_____ 11. Match peers with learners
_____ 12. Train peers
  _____ specify peer tasks
  _____ develop performance criteria statements
  _____ develop training tasks
_____ 13. Manage the peer-learner interaction
  _____ monitor
  _____ apply contingencies
_____ 14. Revise as indicated by the data

37

A Survey of Research

The literature on the role of teacher helpers supports the positive effects of these volunteers in the classroom. For example, volunteers may help individualize instruction (Dineen, Clark, & Risley, 1977; Ellson, Barber, Engle, & Kempworth, 1965; Parson & Heward, 1979) and provide students with more attention and time in classroom instruction (Drabman, Ross, Lynd, & Cordua, 1978; Fixsen, Phillips, & Wolf, 1972; Surratt, Ulrich, & Hawkins, 1969). When paraprofessionals are enlisted, the teacher's time can be used more efficiently (Bailey, Timbers, Phillips, & Wolf, 1971; Robertson, DeReus, & Drabman, 1976; Willis, Morris, & Crowder, 1972). Additionally, research suggests that students can learn many skills from teacher helpers (Harris & Sherman, 1973; Jason, Ferone, & Soucy, 1969; Walker & Buckley, 1972).

Data on the recruitment and selection of volunteers are limited, but they suggest that potential volunteers be clearly informed regarding job requirements and positive and negative aspects of the working environment (Mass, 1978; Rowe, 1976; Wanous, 1973; Weitz, 1958). Hart and King (1979) investigated the selection of paraprofessional counselors. Their results indicated that systematic training resulted in the same level of functioning on follow-up measures regardless of initial "helping" skill (e.g., listening, summarizing) performance. Similar results were reported by Ehly and Larsen (1976). However, conflicting evidence was presented by Carkhuff (1969), who examined the process of selecting paraprofessionals in the helping professions. He concluded that high levels of "helping" skills prior to specific training were an important factor in selecting aides. It also has been shown that having someone *demonstrate* that they can do a task is almost always more accurate in predicting final performance than asking them if they can do it (Biersner & Ryman, 1974; Campion, 1975; Dunnette & Borman, 1979).

The need for systematic training and continued management of paraprofessionals has been discussed by a variety of researchers (Brethower, 1972; Fixsen et al., 1972; Martin, 1972; Patterson & Fagot, 1967; Strain, Shores, & Timm, 1977; Quilitch, 1975). Careful training is well worth the effort: when tutors learn new skills, for example, the students they tutor improve more rapidly (Greenwood, Sloane, & Baskin, 1974; Johnson & Bailey, 1974; Solomon & Wahler, 1973). Training strategies found in the literature include basic modeling, rehearsal, verbal instruction, feedback, and prompting procedures (Jason et al., 1969; Kazdin, 1973; Sepler & Myers, 1978).

Studies that demonstrate the effect school principals can have on student performance are also reported in the literature. In an early study Brown, Copeland, and Hall (1972) showed that when a principal delivered tokens plus back up reinforcers to those students arriving in class on time, the chronic tardiness of one boy was eliminated. In a follow-up study, Copeland, Brown, and Hall (1974) extended this idea to modify the performance of an entire classroom. The authors found that use of contingent principal attention helped improve the academic performance of students in two third grade classrooms. Darch and Thorpe (1977) demonstrated that with only about 2 minutes of principal attention contingent upon the appropriate social and academic behavior of a class of fourth grade students, on-task behavior could be dramatically increased. The principal's attention was administered through a procedure referred to as the Principal's Game. In another study, Thorpe, Darch, and Drecktrah (1978) demonstrated that when the principal made phone calls to the parents of students who demonstrated appropriate social and academic behavior, there was a dramatic improvement in the performance of five disruptive third grade students. Finally, Thorpe, Drecktrah, and Darch (1979) studied the effectiveness of the principal's phone calls to parents of seventh grade students. Again the study demonstrated the powerful effect principal involvement in the school process can have on students' performance.

Experimenters have documented positive results achieved by students who were taught academic, social, and employment skills by peers and older classmates (Clarke, Greenwood, Abramowitz, & Bellamy, 1980; Dineen et al., 1977; Drabman, 1973; Strain, Cooke, & Apolloni, 1976). The teaching skill of peer volunteers has been demonstrated when peers have been trained to present instructional material systematically (Niedermeyer, 1970; Parson & Heward, 1979) and to manage classroom behavior (Greenwood et al., 1974; Solomon & Wahler, 1973). In fact, both peer tutors and their pupils have been shown to make academic gains when teaching is in content areas. For example, Chiang, Thorpe, and Darch (1980) demonstrated that learning disabled peer tutors increased their word reading ability by tutoring less skilled learning disabled students. All tutees improved their performance on reading morphemes, while all tutors showed impressive gains in reading multi-syllabic words containing one or more of the morphemes they had taught. In this study, it was clear that cross-age tutoring can be mutually beneficial. Other studies have supported the position that cross-age tutoring can provide valuable assistance to classroom teachers who often face heavy student demands for individual attention (Epstein, 1978; Jenkins, Mayhall, Peschka, & Jenkins, 1974; Lewis, 1979).

References

Bailey, J. A., Timbers, G. D., Phillips, E. L., & Wolf, M. M. Modification of articulation errors of pre-delinquents by their peers. *Journal of Applied Behavior Analysis*, 1971, 4, 265-281.

Biersner, R. J., & Ryman, D. H. Prediction of job training performance. *Journal of Applied Psychology*, 1974, *59*, 519-521.

Brethower, D. N. *Behavioral analysis in business and industry: A total performance system*. Kalamazoo, Mich.: Behaviordelia, 1972.

Brown, R. E., Copeland, R. E., & Hall, V. R. The school principal as a behavior modifier. *The Journal of Educational Research*, 1972, *66*, 175-180.

Campion, W. F. Accuracy of verifiable biographical information blank responses. *Journal of Applied Psychology*, 1975, *60*, 767-769.

Carkhuff, R. R. *Helping and human relations: A primer for lay professional helpers* (Vols. 1 and 2). New York: Holt, Rinehart & Winston, 1969.

Chiang, B., Thorpe, H., & Darch, C. Effects of cross-age tutoring on word recognition performance of learning disabled students. *Learning Disability Quarterly*, 1980, *3*, 11-19.

Clarke, J. Y., Greenwood, L., Abramowitz, D., & Bellamy, G. T. Summer jobs for vocational preparation of moderately and severely retarded adolescents. In R. H. Horner & G. T. Bellamy (Eds.), *Habilitation of severely and profoundly retarded adults* (Vol. III). Eugene, Oreg.: Specialized Training Program, University of Oregon, 1980. (Monograph No. 3)

Copeland, R. E., Brown, R. E., & Hall, V. R. The effects of principal implemented techniques on the behavior of pupils. *Journal of Applied Behavior Analysis*, 1974, *7*, 77-86.

Darch, C. B., & Thorpe, H. W. The principal game: A group consequence procedure to increase on-task behavior. *Psychology in the Schools*, 1977, *14*, 341-347.

Dineen, J. P., Clark, H. B., & Risley, T. R. Peer tutoring among elementary students: Educational benefits to the tutor. *Journal of Applied Behavior Analysis*, 1977, *10*, 231-238.

Drabman, R. S. Child- versus teacher-administered token programs in a psychiatric hospital school. *Journal of Abnormal Child Psychology*, 1973, *1*, 68-87.

Drabman, R. S., Ross, J. M., Lynd, R. S., & Cordua, G. D. Retarded children as observers, mediators, and generalization programmers using an icing procedure. *Behavior Modification*, 1978, *2*, 371-385.

Dunnette, M. D., & Borman, W. C. Personnel selection and classification systems. *Annual Review of Psychology*, 1979, *30*, 477-525.

Ehly, S., & Larsen, S. Tutor and tutee characteristics as predictors of tutorial outcomes. *Psychology in the Schools*, 1976, *13*, 348-349.

Ellson, D. G., Barber, L., Engle, T. L., & Kempworth, L. Programed tutoring: A teaching aid and a research tool. *Reading Research Quarterly*, 1965, *1*, 77-127.

Epstein, L. The effects of interclass peer tutoring on the vocabulary development of learning disabled students. *Journal of Learning Disabilities*, 1978, *11*, 518-521.

Fixsen, D. L., Phillips, E. L., & Wolf, M. M. Achievement Place: The reliability of self-reporting and peer-reporting and their effects on behavior. *Journal of Applied Behavior Analysis*, 1972, *5*, 19-30.

Greenwood, C. R., Sloane, H. N., & Baskin, A. Training elementary aged peer-behavior managers to control small group programmed mathematics. *Journal of Applied Behavior Analysis*, 1974, *7*, 103-114.

Harris, V. W., & Sherman, J. A. Effects of peer tutoring and consequences on the math performance of elementary classroom students. *Journal of Applied Behavior Analysis*, 1973, *6*, 587-597.

Hart, L. E., & King, G. D. Selection versus training in the development of paraprofessionals. *Journal of Counseling Psychology*, 1979, *26*, 235-241.

Jason, L. A., Ferone, L., & Soucy, G. Teaching peer-tutoring behaviors in first- and third-grade classrooms. *Psychology in the Schools*, 1969, *16*, 261-269.

Jenkins, J. R., Mayhall, W. F., Peschka, C. M., & Jenkins, L. M. Comparing small-group and tutorial instruction in resource rooms. *Exceptional Children*, 1974, *41*, 245-250.

Johnson, M., & Bailey, J. S. Cross-age tutoring: Fifth graders as arithmetic tutors for kindergarten children. *Journal of Applied Behavior Analysis*, 1974, *7*, 223-232.

Kazdin, A. E. The effect of vicarious reinforcement on attentive behavior in the classroom. *Journal of Applied Behavior Analysis*, 1973, *6*, 71-78.

Lewis, J. M. Analysis of the tutoring variable in individualized instruction. *Educational Technology*, 1979, *19*, 41-45.

Martin, G. L. Teaching operant technology to psychiatric nurses, aides and attendants. In F. W. Clark, D. R. Evans, & L. A. Hamerlynck (Eds.), *Implementing behavioral programs for schools*. Champaign, Ill.: Research Press, 1972.

Mass, N. A. Managerial recruitment and attrition: A policy. *Behavioral Science*, 1978, *23*, 49-60.

Niedermeyer, F. C. Effects of training on the instructional behaviors of student tutors. *The Journal of Educational Research*, 1970, *64*, 119.

Parson, L. R., & Heward, W. L. Training peers to tutor: Evaluation of a tutor training package for primary learning disabled students. *Journal of Applied Behavior Analysis*, 1979, *12*, 309-310.

Patterson, G. R., & Fagot, B. Selective responsiveness to social reinforcers and deviant behavior in children. *Psychological Record*, 1967, *17*, 369-378.

Quilitch, H. R. A comparison of three staff-management procedures. *Journal of Applied Behavior Analysis*, 1975, *8*, 59-66.

Robertson, S. J., DeReus, D. M., & Drabman, R. S. Peer and college-student tutoring as reinforcement in a token economy. *Journal of Applied Behavior Analysis*, 1976, *9*, 169-177.

Rowe, P. Effects of expected job characteristics and interview factors on organizational choice. *Psychological Reports*, 1976, *38*, 1011-1018.

Sepler, H. J., & Myers, S. L. The effectiveness of verbal instruction on teaching behavior modification skills to non-professionals. *Journal of Applied Behavior Analysis*, 1978, *11*, 198.

Silbert, J., Carnine, D., & Stein, M. *Direct Instruction Mathematics*. Columbus, Ohio: Charles E. Merrill, 1981.

Solomon, R. W., & Wahler, R. G. Peer reinforcement control of classroom problem behavior. *Journal of Applied Behavior Analysis*, 1973, *6*, 49-56.

Strain, P. S., Cooke, T. P., & Apolloni, T. The role of peers in modifying classmate social behavior: A review. *Journal of Special Education*, 1976, *10*, 351-356.

Strain, P. S., Shores, R. E., & Timm, M. A. Effects of peer social initiations on the behavior of withdrawn preschool children. *Journal of Applied Behavior Analysis*, 1977, *10*, 289-298.

Surratt, P. R., Ulrich, R. E., & Hawkins, R. P. An elementary student as a behavioral engineer. *Journal of Applied Behavior Analysis*, 1969, *2*, 85-92.

Thorpe, H. W., Darch, C. B., & Drecktrah, M. The principal lottery: A system utilizing contingent principal phone calls to increase on-task behavior. *Corrective and Social Psychiatry and Journal of Behavior Technology Methods and Therapy*, 1978, *24*, 20-24.

Thorpe, H., Drecktrah, M., & Darch, C. The principal lottery revisited in a middle school classroom. *Corrective and Social Psychiatry and Journal of Behavior Technology Methods and Therapy*, 1979, *25*, 86-90.

Walker, H. M., & Buckley, N. K. Programming generalization and maintenance of treatment effects across time and across settings. *Journal of Applied Behavior Analysis*, 1972, *5*, 209-224.

Wanous, J. P. Effects of a realistic job preview on job acceptance, job attitudes, and job survival. *Journal of Applied Psychology*, 1973, *58*, 327-332.

Weitz, J. Job expectancy and survival. *Journal of Applied Psychology*, 1958, *40*, 245-247.

Willis, J. W., Morris, B., & Crowder, J. A remedial reading technique for disabled readers that employs students as behavioral engineers. *Psychology in the Schools*, 1972, *9*, 67-70.

Chapter 4

Using Your Attention to Manage Student Behavior

The attention you give to students is one of the most powerful ways you have of managing their behavior. However, you must use it carefully so that it works *for* you and not *against* you.

Why Use Special Procedures to Guide Your Attention?

In one actual classroom situation, a teacher tried to keep her students under control by reprimanding them when they misbehaved. Like most children, these students valued the teacher's attention, even though it was mostly negative, and were willing to do whatever was necessary to have her notice them. Since she only paid attention when they misbehaved or broke the rules, they began acting up and breaking the rules more often. The more they misbehaved, the more she paid attention to them; and the more she paid attention to them, the more they acted up. They were caught in an endless negative cycle.

Finally, someone else observed what was happening and suggested that the teacher redirect her attention, providing it for positive, rather than negative, behavior. The change worked wonders. It took time for the students to realize what was required of them to receive the teacher's attention, but the teacher was persistent—and eventually successful. She ignored mild acting up which seemed to be done just to get her attention, dealt with more troublesome misbehavior by temporarily suspending certain classroom privileges for the violators, and most importantly, gave students considerable attention for following the rules, working accurately, and completing assignments.

This factual anecdote has important implications for the way you use your attention with the students in your classroom. It is clear that teachers cannot afford merely to "act out their feelings" in the classroom—being "grouchy" or "grumpy" when they are tired or feeling out of sorts, and being cheerful and positive when things have been going their way and they are well rested. They must attempt to maintain an even disposition with their students, even on days when it is trying to do so. The effort to be consistent will be rewarded with more consistent behavior from the students.

Special procedures can be used to guide your attention in order to keep students working at consistently high levels of efficiency and to help you make the most effective use of such attention.

Who Can Use Their Attention to Manage Student Behavior?

The procedures described in this chapter are primarily for use by the teacher. However, the procedures also can be employed effectively by aides, volunteers, counselors, principals, and other adults in the school who have been trained to use them.

How to Use Your Attention to Manage Student Behavior

Most often, you will use your attention to manage student behavior while students are involved in seatwork activities. However, you will find that the techniques discussed in this chapter also apply to many other situations in which you interact with students, such as during instructional periods in the classroom, during transition times, during unstructured classroom occasions (before and after school, during free time), in the hallways, on the playground, in the lunchroom, and so on. Whenever and wherever you want to let students know that their behavior matches your expectations, you can use these procedures.

Student Behaviors to Be Noticed

Apply your positive attention to any student behavior that measures up to your standards in the classroom or elsewhere in school. If you see students following the rules, let them know that you have noticed and that you appreciate their efforts. If you see students working carefully, handing in a completed paper, checking their work, being kind to someone else, cooperating with others, or doing virtually anything else in school that you would like to encourage or that you feel *needs* encouragement, let the students know that you have noticed.

Students sometimes play a game with teachers, principals, or other authorities, glancing around quickly to see if anyone is watching before they do something they know they should not do. You can play a game of your own with them. Glance around the room discreetly every now and then and surprise students who are behaving well by acknowledging their efforts. It will short-circuit the games students play with you, win them over to your side, and encourage them to work hard in an effort to gain your positive attention.

Component Skills Involved in Using Your Attention

There are four component skills involved in using your attention to improve students' behavior: moving, scanning, praising, and following up on previous efforts to manage students' behavior.

1. *Moving*. In this context, moving simply means moving slowly but steadily about the room while students perform independent seatwork activities. This recommendation assumes that you are not involved in other teaching activities during this time.

Moving should be done in an unpredictable pattern. Otherwise, students will learn when you are going to be near them and begin working only as you approach. If your movement is random, students will be encouraged to work more steadily. The process of moving involves many stops as you pause to look at a student's work, answer a question, or help a student momentarily with a difficult task. But these pauses should be brief, or other students in the room may stop working when they feel your attention is focused elsewhere. When you stop, try to start moving again, or at least glance up, within 15 to 20 or (at the most) 30 seconds. When you begin moving again, you do not need to continue in the same direction. It's a good idea to change directions now and then to avoid falling into a predictable pattern.

2. *Scanning*. Scanning goes hand in hand with moving and stopping, and it sets the stage for the next skill—praising students who are doing well. To scan, simply look around the room at various students while you are moving—and glance around the room when you stop. It keeps you continuously aware of what any student in the class is doing at a given time and gives you an instant impression of how the class as a whole is behaving.

Scanning can involve a "sweep" of the entire room or a series of repeating "spot checks" of various segments of the room. "Sweeping" the room with your eyes should be done slowly at first, and "spot checks" of various zones of the room should be held momentarily until you learn to tell in an instant what the students are doing when you look at them. Although this seems simple, it is easy to get fooled. Many students are experts at looking busy while actually being off-task, or even disruptive, in very subtle ways. Don't let yourself be fooled by them. If you are, they will learn quickly that they can get by with certain things in your class, and they will begin to test the limits of your awareness and your tolerance. If you are not convinced that students are actually working, move closer until you can tell for certain. As you practice this skill, you will become adept at judging quickly whether students are doing what you expect of them at any given moment.

3. *Praising*. Skillful praising is the essence of using your attention effectively to manage student behavior. It involves noticing when students are doing well; calling out their names publicly or speaking to them privately (whichever is most appropriate to their age and ability level); and describing clearly, but briefly, the behavior you want to encourage (e.g., "Steve, you went from one page right to the next; that's the way to keep working!" or "Janice, you capitalized the first word of every sentence; you've really learned the rule!").

4. *Following up*. Sometimes you can praise one or two students in order to communicate indirectly to another student to return to work. Most of the time you do not want to provide direct attention to students who are dawdling, whispering to a neighbor, and so on, since to do so might turn into a negative cycle for you just as it did for the teacher described earlier in this chapter. You can avoid this cycle by ignoring minor inappropriate behavior and instead praising nearby students who are working appropriately. This tactic is referred to as "praising around" the misbehavior. When you use this technique, you should glance discreetly at the student who was misbehaving to see if the pupil has gone back to work yet and, if so, praise the student for returning to the task. This practice of watching students to catch them working, then praising them for their behavior is what we refer to as "following up" on the indirect communication to return to work.

Characteristics of effective praise. Effective praising is characterized by several important features.

1. *Good praise follows the "if-then rule."* The "if-then rule" states that *if* the student is doing something you want to encourage—something you want to see the student do again or do more often in the future (and if you are sure that that is what the student is doing)—*then* (and *only* then) you should praise the student for it. Following this rule to the letter is extremely important in influencing student behavior in the manner you intend to influence it.

Timing is a critical element in making the "if-then rule" work for you when encouraging a student behavior you observe. If it is a fleeting behavior (such as saying "Thank you" to someone), make your praise statement to the student within 1 or 2 seconds after the behavior occurs. If it is an on-going action (such as reading quietly to oneself), immediately praise the student *during* the behavior. Remember: be *sure* students are actually doing what you are ready to praise them for, and once sure, offer your praise within 1 or 2 seconds. If you follow these two components of the "if-then rule," you will increase your chances of successfully influencing student behavior.

2. *Good praise often includes students' names.* With younger students, you can often get considerable efficiency out of your attention by praising "publicly." This means praising out loud or calling out praise statements to students who are some distance away from you. When you praise publicly, it is important to call out the names of the students you are praising so your attention "hits home" and has the desired effect. If you simply say, "That's the way to work over there, you guys," and if one student "over there" is not actually working, you risk the possibility of praising that student for the wrong behavior. But if you say, "Peter and Susan, that's the way to work," there is no question about who is being praised.

With older students, especially those in the intermediate grades, public praise sometimes will not work. If students tease each other about getting the teacher's attention or being the "teacher's pet," or if they mimic your praise comments in a sarcastic tone of voice, you should limit your use of public praise. Instead, praise students privately by speaking softly or whispering to the student when you are nearby. When you do this, using the student's name probably is not necessary to ensure that the communication gets through to the right student. Still, it is a nice touch, since many students like to hear adults call them by their first name.

3. *Good praise is descriptive.* The sample praise statements we have used so far all have one thing in common: they describe the student behavior the teacher wants to encourage. Many people have a natural tendency to *evaluate* the children rather than *describe* what they are doing. Evaluative comments refer to a person's characteristics and use verbs such as "is" and "are": "He *is* mean," "They *are* cooperative," "She *is* nice." Descriptive comments simply *describe* what the student is doing at any given time—focusing on actions—and use words like "did" and other action verbs: "You *did* that assignment really quickly," "You *worked* the whole period," "You *answered* all the problems correctly." Descriptive praise effectively communicates to students what you want them to do. Evaluative praise communicates less clearly; it focuses too much on the child and not enough on what the child does. Remember to praise the *behavior* and not the child.

4. *Good praise is convincing.* Good praise convinces the student that you really mean what you say. When praising younger students, try to sound enthusiastic; put expression into your voice and vary your tone rather than using a flat or monotone voice. However, with older students—perhaps beginning with second or third graders—enthusiastic praise begins to sound artificial or "gushy." For this age group, you will

need to convince students of your sincerity in other ways. Moderate your tone to convey that you are impressed with their work, but make your praise more subtle than you would with younger students. Address your praise more to the *end results* of their work than to the *process* of working. Continue to use their names when you praise students, but do so more privately and quietly. These guidelines will help convince students that your praise is sincere.

5. *Good praise is varied.* To avoid having your praise statements become empty, tiresome, and ineffective, vary them by praising different students for different things, depending on what they most need encouragement for. Describe different features of students' work that you want to acknowledge (e.g., neatness, accuracy, completion). Also, use variety in the wording of the praise. Do not make all of your praise statements sound like "so-and-so did this," "so-and-so did that," and "someone else did the other thing." Sometimes you can simply state what the student did. Other times you can say, "Thank you for doing _____"; and still other times you can say, "I appreciate the way you _____" or "I like the way you _____." In short, you can use different types of statements to vary your praise. Each statement can include the student's name and the behavior you are praising.

6. *Good praise is nondisruptive.* If you find that your public praise seems disruptive to students the first few days that you start using it, you should not be concerned. Initially, students might look up from their work at you, look at the student being praised, or giggle when you praise out loud. If the praise continues to disrupt students after a week of trying the procedures, however, you can simply tell the students that sometimes you will be talking out loud when they are working, and that when you do so, they should continue to work unless you are talking specifically to them or to the whole class. You can also praise students who do *not* look up, look around, or giggle when you praise others. If this doesn't work, you might try toning down your praise a little, making it less loud or *slightly* less enthusiastic. This problem probably will not arise with older students, whom you praise more privately. If it does, it can be handled in the same way.

Useful types of praise. There are four types of praise you will find helpful in managing your classroom. They are (1) nearby praise, (2) across-the-room praise, (3) praise while helping, and (4) praise while teaching.

1. *Nearby praise.* Nearby praise is delivered to students when you are near them. You can use it when circulating around the room, when standing next to students who are lining up, or with a group of students

anywhere in the room. It can be delivered privately or publicly to one student or to several students at once.

2. *Across-the-room praise.* Across-the-room praise is called out to students who are some distance away from you. By definition, it is public praise. However, simply because the praise is public does not mean you cannot use it with older students. In such cases, you can tailor the content and the voice tone of the comment to the level of the students.

Part of the value of across-the-room praise lies in the fact it can be used in conjunction with scanning and glancing around the room. Such praise communicates to students who are some distance away that you are still aware of what they are doing, even though you are not near them. Thus, it is a valuable technique for keeping students working without being next to them.

3. *Praise while helping.* Praise while helping involves glancing up from your work when you are tutoring or otherwise helping a student and praising one or more other students who are working several feet away. It is actually a special kind of praising across the room. Thus, it is also public praise.

Observation in some classrooms shows that when teachers hold their attention with a student they are helping for more than 15 to 20 seconds, other students in the room stop working, one by one. Within as little as 2 minutes, many students might be off-task or even disruptive. While this situation is not uncommon, it can be prevented easily. Simply look up from your tutoring every 15 to 20 or 30 seconds and praise two or three students who are still working. By doing so, you can keep students on-task and show them you are aware of what they are doing, even though you are helping someone else. This technique can encourage students to develop good work habits. Eventually, you will be able to praise less often and still keep the students working.

4. *Praise while teaching.* Praise while teaching is both a special kind of across-the-room praise and praise while helping. It involves praising students who are at their desks or in some other part of the room while you are conducting lessons with a group of students.

In training teachers to conduct direct small-group instruction, we found that they tended to devote all their attention to the students in their small group and ignore the other students in the room. We know that students who are not supervised often get out of control quickly. Thus, we would sometimes see effective small-group instruction being conducted in the midst of a chaotic classroom. It takes considerable skill to both do a good job of teaching small groups and maintain control in the classroom. However, we found that teachers could do so quite easily

if we simply asked them to glance up from their small-group work periodically (such as at the end of a task or at the end of a page), glance around
the room, and call out a praise comment to two or three students who
were doing what was expected of them. The practice of praising some
students while teaching others only requires 3 to 5 seconds of the
teacher's time to carry out, but seems to pay enormous dividends in
terms of overall classroom control and the development of good work
habits by students who are not closely supervised.

The following checklist shows how to begin using the procedures
described in this chapter and how to modify them later in the school
year. It can also be used as a reminder of how and when to praise. Similar
checklists will appear throughout the book at the conclusion of the discussion for each procedure.

Using Your Attention to Manage Student Behavior
Implementation Checklist

Early Year

(First day of school until student behavior is consistently good and for 1
to 2 days after any vacation)

1. During at least part of each seatwork period of the day, circulate
   among the students. Move in an unpredictable pattern, scanning
   the room, and praise students for following the seatwork rules and
   for other appropriate behaviors. Be sure your comments have the
   characteristics of effective praise:

   ■ Follow the "if-then rule."
   ■ Use the students' names.
   ■ Describe student behavior.
   ■ Show enthusiasm.
   ■ Use variety.
   ■ Be nondisruptive.

   If you praise around a student, be sure to follow up with praise if
   the child begins working.

2. Use each of the following praise types during each circulation
   period: nearby praise, across-the-room praise, and praise while
   helping. Use praise while teaching when conducting small-group
   instruction.

Mid- and Late Year

(After student behavior is consistently good, continuing until the end of
the school year)

1. Circulate and praise during at least one seatwork period daily. You
   might want to circulate during more periods for purposes of tutoring and correcting problems as you circulate.

2. Continue to use each of the various types of praise, but try to praise
   less often without getting a decrease in student performance. Adjust your praise level to student behavior. As a general rule, *praise
   more when students have trouble working; praise less when they
   are doing well.*

A Survey of Research

Positive teacher attention seems to be a very natural part of teaching, but some research shows that it is not always used as extensively or as appropriately as it might be. White (1975) showed that teachers attend to students at moderate levels in the first two grades and that a majority of this recognition is positive attention for desirable behavior. But beginning in third grade, and continuing progressively through twelfth grade, levels of teacher attention to student behavior drop off sharply; more attention is paid to undesirable behavior than to students' appropriate conduct. Similar findings were reported by Thomas, Presland, Grant, and Glynn (1978). This picture suggests that we need to make deliberate efforts to praise often enough to keep students working well and that we need to guard against the tendency to attend to minor misbehavior.

Many researchers have investigated the potential effects of positive teacher attention across a variety of student ages, behaviors, and settings and found it to be an extremely versatile technique. In particular, praise has been shown to be an effective procedure for preschoolers (Buell, Stoddard, Harris, & Baer, 1968), primary grade children (Broden, Bruce, Mitchell, Carter, & Hall, 1970), intermediate grade students (Luiselli & Downing, 1980), and junior high school adolescents (Kirby & Shields, 1972). It has been shown to affect both on-task and academic performance measures (Kirby & Shields, 1972) as well as students' social interaction (Hart, Reynolds, Baer, Brawley, & Harris, 1968).

Although much of the published literature on the use of praise documents its effects only with one child or a small group of students at one time, program descriptions are also available that illustrate how praise can be used effectively with an entire classroom of youngsters (e.g., Hopkins & Conard, 1976). Similarly, teacher praise on a classroom-wide basis has been shown to correlate positively with student achievement in the elementary grades (Cantrell, Stenner, & Katzenmeyer, 1977; Good, Ebmeier, & Beckerman, 1978). The chapter by Hopkins and Conard in *Teaching Special Children* (1976) is an excellent—and highly readable— account of the powerful potential of teacher praise. It provides much of the basis for procedures recommended in this chapter.

Praise is seldom used in isolation from other student management procedures. It is often combined with rules (see Chapter 5 in this volume), with ignoring or loss of privileges for mildly inappropriate behavior (Chapter 10), and with point systems and/or activity reinforcers (Chapter 11). Madsen, Becker, and Thomas (1968) found that for rules or ignoring to be effective, they had to be combined with praise. These authors called praise "the key to effective classroom management." Virtually every researcher who has investigated such classroom management procedures as point systems, point fines or loss of privileges, or activity reinforcers has used them in combination with praise. Praise is the procedure that makes behavior reduction techniques, such as ignoring or loss of privileges, educative and not simply punitive. Especially when it is descriptive, praise provides an educational function, *teaching* students what is expected of them, as opposed to merely punishing them when they stray from the rules.

Praise has also been shown to affect the behavior of students near those being praised. In one study (Broden et al., 1970), praise delivered to one student was shown to increase attending behavior in a student sitting at an adjacent desk.

Finally, it is possible that the use of praise can enhance students' self-concepts. It seems plausible that students' self-concepts are formed partially by what they hear about themselves from significant people in their environment. If this is true, praise is even more important than we have already indicated in this chapter.

References

Broden, M., Bruce, C., Mitchell, M., Carter, V., & Hall, R. V. Effects of teacher attention on attending behavior of two boys at adjacent desks. *Journal of Applied Behavior Analysis*, 1970, *3*, 205-211.

Buell, J., Stoddard, P., Harris, F., & Baer, D. Collateral social development accompanying reinforcement of outdoor play in a preschool child. *Journal of Applied Behavior Analysis*, 1968, *1*, 167-173.

Cantrell, R., Stenner, A., & Katzenmeyer, W. Teacher knowledge, attitudes, and classroom teaching correlates of student achievement. *Journal of Educational Psychology*, 1977, *69*, 172-179.

Good, T., Ebmeier, H., & Beckerman, T. Teaching mathematics in high and low SES classrooms: An experimental comparison. *Journal of Teacher Education*, 1978, *29*, 85-90.

Hart, B., Reynolds, N., Baer, D., Brawley, E., & Harris, F. Effect of contingent and noncontingent social reinforcement on the cooperative play of a preschool child. *Journal of Applied Behavior Analysis*, 1968, *1*, 73-76.

Hopkins, R. L., & Conard, R. Putting it all together: Super school. In N. Haring and R. Schiefelbusch (Eds.), *Teaching special children*. New York: McGraw-Hill, 1976.

Kirby, F., & Shields, F. Modification of arithmetic response rate and attending behavior in a seventh-grade student. *Journal of Applied Behavior Analysis*, 1972, *5*, 79-84.

Luiselli, J., & Downing, J. Improving a student's arithmetic performance using feedback and reinforcement procedures. *Education and Treatment of Children*, 1980, *3*, 45-49.

Madsen, C., Becker, W., & Thomas, D. Rules, praise, and ignoring: Elements of elementary classroom control. *Journal of Applied Behavior Analysis*, 1968, *1*, 139-150.

Thomas, J., Presland, I., Grant, M., & Glynn, T. Natural rates of teacher approval and disapproval in grade-7 classrooms. *Journal of Applied Behavior Analysis*, 1978, *11*, 91-94.

White, M. Natural rates of teacher approval and disapproval in the classroom. *Journal of Applied Behavior Analysis*, 1975, *8*, 367-372.

Chapter 5

Establishing and Implementing
Classroom Rules

Classroom rules are an important part of the overall classroom management process. Yet to be truly effective, rules cannot merely be posted and forgotten; they should serve as a framework for guiding both the students' and the teacher's behavior throughout the year.

Why Establish Classroom Rules?

Classroom rules serve several important functions. First, rules communicate the teacher's expectations regarding student behavior in the classroom. If the students are allowed to participate in the rule-making process, the rules communicate their expectations for each other as well. Once the rules have been established and taught to the class, students cannot say that they didn't know about a rule and therefore can't be held responsible for observing it. Only by actively teaching what the rules are and how to follow them can teachers be fair in their classroom management efforts.

A second reason to establish clear classroom rules is to provide a basis for the teacher to "catch the students being good." While the old saying goes, "Rules are made to be broken," in the classroom model described in this book, rules are made to be followed. The teacher is the one who must show students how to follow them. Rules alone usually do not provide enough structure to keep students out of trouble; students need to receive attention occasionally for observing the rules. Procedures for catching the students following the rules, and acknowledging them for it, are described in Chapter 4, "Using Your Attention to Manage Student Behavior."

Who Is Involved in Establishing and Implementing
Classroom Rules?

We recommend that both the teacher and the students participate in establishing rules for the classroom. As the teacher, you should decide before the school year begins what kinds of situations should be covered by rules and what kinds of rules should be in effect in each situation. (Some procedures in this book rely on the use of certain rules to be effective. Such rules are listed in subsequent chapters.) You can then have students help you develop these rules, discussing them and asking for additions or suggested wording. Finally, you need to help students learn how to keep the rules. This step involves teaching the rules, providing attention when you "catch" students following them, and helping the students support and remind each other about the rules.

One point to keep in mind: student-made rules often are more strict than those set down by teachers. As a result, we recommend that you have a clear idea of what rules you want to have in effect in your classroom before you conduct a rules discussion with the students. We also suggest that you moderate the students' rule-making efforts so that they do not become unrealistic. Rules that set behavior standards too high soon will be discarded. On the other hand, students' behavior tends to be only as good as the standards you set. Thus, you will need to lead the students gently in the direction of the rules that you identified before the year began.

By participating in the process, students will see these rules as *their* own and not merely as standards someone else has imposed on them. Students should also have the opportunity to describe what they consider to be "ideal" conduct for themselves and what expectations they have for the behavior of their classmates.

How to Establish and Implement Classroom Rules

This section presents guidelines for developing and implementing effective classroom rules. By following these guidelines carefully, we believe that you and your students can devise rules that will help structure your classroom for success. You are likely to find that students not only learn better in a more structured classroom but actually prefer it over a less structured and unpredictable environment.

Characteristics of Good Rules

Follow these suggestions to formulate reasonable and workable classroom rules.

1. *Keep the rules to a minimum for any given classroom situation.* We recommend using no more than three or four rules for any given activity. Students will have difficulty remembering more than this. If you feel that you need more coverage than four rules allow, simply state the rules a little more broadly.

2. *Keep the wording of the rules simple.* This will help the students remember them and will help you make praise comments to the students based on the wording of the rules.

3. *State the rules positively.* That is, state them as *do's*, not as don'ts. For example, instead of saying "No looking around" as a rule for group instruction, say "Keep your eyes on the teacher." The second statement tells them what to *do*, rather than what to avoid doing, and is thus more instructive.

4. *Use different rules for different situations if you find this helpful.* Sometimes it is difficult to establish one set of rules that adequately covers all the classroom situations you might want to structure. For example, you might find that the rules you have established for group instruction do not apply as well to seatwork periods. One solution to this problem is to identify the situations that seem to require their own set of rules and lead the students through the rule-setting process for each one.

5. *Post the rules in a prominent location.* Posted rules act as a reminder to students of the behavior that is expected of them in the classroom. If you have different sets of rules for each of three or four classroom situations, you should post the rules near each activity. For example, rules for instructional periods can be placed behind the spot where the teacher usually stands or sits when teaching the students; rules for seatwork can be posted on the wall students face when they are seated at their desks.

Establishing the Rules

The best time to establish rules with the students is early in the morning on the *first* day of school. This will let them know that rules are important and will let you start teaching them to follow the rules right away. The process can be structured as a group discussion. As mentioned earlier, you should identify before the school year begins the activities that will be covered by rules (e.g., instructional periods and seatwork) and the kinds of rules that will best structure behavior in each activity.

1. *Tell students the importance of having rules in the classroom.* Rules are needed so all the students will know what is expected of them and discipline will be fair and clearly understood.

2. *Tell the students that you want them to help you write the rules for the classroom.* It is their classroom, their education that is being structured, and you want them to be a part of it. Make it clear that you are the manager of the classroom and that it is your job to teach the rules once they are agreed upon. Let them know that you are willing and able to impose your own rules if they cannot abide by the ones that you create together. In other words, treat this process as the serious and important task it is.

3. *Tell students which classroom activities will need to be covered by rules.* Discuss the activities one at a time and have the students suggest

what kinds of behavior on their part would be most appropriate in each situation. Moderate this discussion so that it remains on the topic and so that students contribute appropriate and realistic ideas. Gently guide the discussion toward the rules you believe would best structure the situation for the students. Write down the rules on the chalkboard as they are suggested, then condense them. You should finish with a list of three or four rules for each situation that reflect your advance planning and the students' input. Make sure the rules you and the students develop conform to the characteristics outlined earlier—they are worded simply, stated positively, and limited to three or four rules for each of the chosen situations.

4. *Once you have refined the rules lists, write each list down on a large piece of tagboard.* Use a Magic Marker so that it can be seen from a distance, then post each list as described before. One way to involve the students in this process is to assign groups of students to the various lists and have them make the charts as a group art project. They can also help choose a spot for each chart and hang the charts up.

Implementing the Rules

Once the rules have been established for each of the classroom activities you intend to structure, teach the rules for a given activity to the students in a 3 to 5 minute "mini-lesson." This is best done just prior to the first time the students take part in each of these activities. For example, before the first instructional period (reading, math, and the like) conduct a brief lesson to teach students the rules that have been established for that type of period. Similarly, just before the first seatwork period to occur after the rules have been posted, teach the seatwork rule statements to the students in a group. Follow this procedure for each of the sets of rules that have been established for your classroom. Sample scripts for presenting and reviewing these lessons are provided at the end of this section. Guidelines for using scripts are found in Chapter 1 under "Learning the Procedures."

Keep in mind that knowing and remembering the rules are not the main goals of teaching them to students. The primary goal is to have students *follow* them. For this reason, it is important to include rule-following practice as part of each "rule" lesson. Even then, the final test is not whether students follow the rules during the rule-training lessons, but whether they observe the rules during the activities. To encourage students to keep the rules in actual situations, you should seek opportunities to "catch" the students following the guidelines established. This idea is similar to the notion of catching students misbehaving, then punishing them, but it is positive rather than negative. Here, you are trying to catch them being good, then rewarding them with your attention in the form of praise, smiles, winks, nods, or a pat on the back. Specific procedures for rewarding students with your attention are described in Chapter 4. Also, encourage students to support one another and remind others about following the rules. In this way, you will be able to foster a spirit of cooperation among your students to support the behaviors most conducive to their success—and yours—in the classroom.

Introducing the Rules with a Script

This script illustrates how you might introduce a set of rules for teacher-led instructional activities. If you establish somewhat different sets of rules for each of three or four classroom situations, you can use similar scripts, simply substituting the rules you are teaching. Thus, the form of the script would remain the same, but the wording would change slightly. Be sure the rules are posted before beginning. In this sample illustration, the rules established are identified first, followed by the script.

Rules for Classroom Instructional Periods	Purpose
1. Watch the teacher and watch your work.	To keep students from looking around the room or looking at others' work
2. Keep your hands and feet to yourself.	To keep students from hitting, pinching, poking, kicking, sprawling
3. Talk only on your turn.	To keep students from talking out of turn

Script for Introducing a Set of Classroom Rules

Teacher	Students
"Today we're going to talk about the rules we developed for our classroom. First we'll talk about what rules we follow when I am teaching a lesson to you." (Point to each rule as you say it.)	
"The first rule for lesson times is, 'Watch the teacher and watch your work.' What is the first rule?" (signal)	"Watch the teacher and watch your work."
"Right. That means that when I am teaching a lesson, you should be either	

Teacher	Students

watching me, or watching the chalk-board, my book, or your workbook, depending on what I ask you to look at."

"Here's the second rule for lesson times: 'Keep your hands and feet to yourself.' What's the second rule?" (signal)

"Keep your hands and feet to yourself."

"That means that during lessons you should keep your hands and feet under control so that you don't accidentally bother anyone else."

"Here's the third rule for lesson times: 'Talk only on your turn.' What's the rule?" (signal)

"Talk only on your turn."

"That means that you should talk when I call on you or when I ask everyone to answer, but not at any other time."

"Now . . . by yourselves." (pause) "Get ready." (Point to each rule as students say it.) (signal)

"Watch the teacher and watch your work. Keep your hands and feet to yourself. Talk only on your turn."

"Very nice. Now let's practice doing what the rules say. I'm going to begin teaching a lesson. I want you to concentrate on following the rules during this practice time, and I'll see who I can catch following each rule we talked about." (Place the rules poster right next to you so that students can see it easily without diverting their attention from you.)

Begin teaching one or two pages from a sample lesson you have selected for this purpose. After every few seconds, praise two or three students for following one of the rules. At first, use the wording of the rule to praise students: "Good, Jean and Jason, you're watching the teacher. That's the way to pay attention" or "Mark and Susan, you're keeping your hands and feet to yourself—way to work." Call on different students each time you

Teacher	Students

praise and refer to different rules. Continue 2 to 3 minutes, then begin your regularly scheduled lesson. Continue to praise rule following, but at a lesser rate.

Repeat this introduction, substituting the appropriate rules, immediately before each of the activities for which you and the students have developed rules. Follow the introduction with 2 to 3 minutes of appropriate practice, such as seatwork practice, transition practice, etc.

Reviewing the Rules with a Script

This script illustrates how to review the rules you introduced to students previously. The script can be modified to review any of the rules you have developed for other activity periods in the classroom. Since rules are created on the first day of school and taught to the students on the first or second day, they should be reviewed on the third, fourth, and fifth days of school, on every Monday for the first month of school, on the first school day following a holiday or vacation of more than 2 days (such as after Thanksgiving, Christmas, or spring break), when a new student joins the class, or whenever else it seems necessary to do so.

Script for Reviewing a Set of Classroom Rules

Teacher	Students
"Today we're going to review the rules in effect when I am teaching a lesson to you." (Point to the chart.)	
"What is the first rule?" (pause) (signal) (Repeat until firm; after the first response, answer with the students, if necessary.)	"Watch the teacher and watch your work."
"What does that mean?" (Call on a single student to describe briefly what the rule means.)	(Student responds in own words.)
"Everybody, what is the first rule?" (signal)	"Watch the teacher and watch your work."
"What is the second rule?" (pause) (signal)	"Keep your hands and feet to yourself."

Teacher	Students
"What does it mean?" (Call on a single student, different than the one who answered previously.)	(Student responds in own words.)
"Everybody, what is the second rule?" (signal)	"Keep your hands and feet to yourself."
"What is the third rule?" (pause) (signal)	"Talk only on your turn."
"What does it mean?" (Call on a third student.)	(Student responds in own words.)
"Everybody, what is the third rule?" (signal)	"Talk only on your turn."
"Good. Let's practice the rules during our lessons, and I'll see who I can catch following them."	
Begin the regularly scheduled lesson. Occasionally praise students who are following various rules.	

For advanced review of any set of rules (by the fourth or fifth day of school and for reviews after the first week of school), you may omit the "What does it mean?" question since, by this time, the students will know the meaning of the rule quite well. Also, you can combine the three rule questions into one: "What are the rules for this activity?" (pause, signal). By then, most students should be able to recite the three rules in sequence. Continue to praise rule following intermittently, even on days when you do not review the rules orally. Direct most of your praise to the students who have the greatest trouble following the rules.

Establishing and Implementing Classroom Rules
Implementation Checklist

Before the First Day of School

1. Decide which activities in your classroom should be covered by rules.
2. Decide what kinds of rules you want to use to structure each activity in your classroom.

On the First Day of School

1. Conduct a group discussion with the students to obtain their suggestions and additions for the sets of classroom rules.
2. Have the students work together in groups to make rules posters to put up in the classroom *or* make the posters yourself after school and put them up before the start of the second day of school.

On the First or Second Day of School

1. Conduct rule-training sessions with students just before beginning the first activity of each type for which you have established rules.
2. Try to catch the students following the rules as often as you can and praise them for doing so.
3. Encourage students to support each other in rule following by reminding each other of the rules for an activity before it begins and by thanking each other for following the rules.

On Subsequent Days of School

1. Review the rules with the students each Monday for the first few weeks of school, on the first day of school following a holiday or vacation (state education association conferences, parent-teacher conferences, Thanksgiving, Christmas, etc.), or whenever it seems necessary.
2. Continue to catch students following the rules several times each day and reward them with your attention.
3. Continue to encourage students to support each other in rule following.

A Survey of Research

The general consensus in published research regarding use of rules in classroom management is that rules alone will not develop and maintain appropriate student behavior (Greenwood, Hops, Delquadri, & Guild, 1974). However, they *are* effective when combined with teacher praise for desirable behavior and ignoring of mildly undesirable responses (Madsen, Becker, & Thomas, 1968; O'Leary, Becker, Evans, & Saudargas, 1969). In all three studies cited, rules were first implemented alone following a baseline phase to determine typical levels of student work-related behaviors in elementary school classrooms. In each case, the rules produced little or no improvement in the students' behavior. When ignoring and praise (Madsen et al., 1968) or a point system (Greenwood et al., 1974; O'Leary et al., 1969) was added to the rule structure, students' behavior improved to acceptable levels. These findings do not support the use of rules in isolation from other management procedures, but suggest that rules provide a logical framework upon which to superimpose consequences for student behavior.

Allowing students to participate in generating rules for their classrooms is supported by a separate line of research. Several investigators (Dickerson & Creedon, 1981; Felixbrod & O'Leary, 1973, 1974) have studied the relative effects of student-selected versus teacher-imposed standards for students' classroom performance. Their findings, as well as those of other researchers (Brownell, Colletti, Ersner-Hershfield, Hershfield, & Wilson, 1977; Glynn, Thomas, & Shee, 1973), show that student-imposed standards are at least as effective as those determined by teachers. One study (Lovitt & Curtis, 1969) found that student-developed standards were *more* effective than those of the teacher. This line of research suggests that not only might students be willing to participate in their own classroom management, they also might benefit behaviorally from this process.

References

Brownell, K., Colletti, G., Ersner-Hershfield, R., Hershfield, S., & Wilson, G. Self-control in school children: Stringency and leniency in self-determined and externally imposed performance standards. *Behavior Therapy*, 1977, *8*, 442-455.

Dickerson, E. A., & Creedon, C. F. Self-selection of standards by children: The relative effectiveness of pupil-selected and teacher-selected standards of performance. *Journal of Applied Behavior Analysis*, 1981, *14*, 425-433.

Felixbrod, J., & O'Leary, K. Effects of reinforcement on children's academic behavior as a function of self-determined and externally imposed contingencies. *Journal of Applied Behavior Analysis*, 1973, *6*, 241-250.

Felixbrod, J., & O'Leary, K. Self-determination of academic standards by children: Toward freedom from external control. *Journal of Educational Psychology*, 1974, *66*, 845-850.

Glynn, E., Thomas, J., & Shee, S. Behavioral self-control of on-task behavior in an elementary classroom. *Journal of Applied Behavior Analysis*, 1973, *6*, 105-113.

Greenwood, C., Hops, H., Delquadri, J., & Guild, J. Group contingencies for group consequences in classroom management: A further analysis. *Journal of Applied Behavior
Analysis*, 1974, *7*, 413-425.

Lovitt, T., & Curtis, K. Academic response rate as a function of teacher- and self-imposed
contingencies. *Journal of Applied Behavior Analysis*, 1969, *2*, 49-53.

Madsen, C. H., Becker, W. C., & Thomas, D. R. Rules, praise, and ignoring: Elements of
elementary classroom control. *Journal of Applied Behavior Analysis*, 1968, *1*, 139-150.

O'Leary, K., Becker, W., Evans, M., & Saudargas, R. A token reinforcement program in a public school: A replication and systematic analysis. *Journal of Applied Behavior Analysis*, 1969, *2*, 3-13.

Chapter 6
Managing Time in the Classroom

How teachers perceive time and how they manage it have a great deal to do with their success in the classroom. In this chapter—and throughout this volume—we make two basic assumptions about time:

1. Time is *like* money. It cannot be recalled or payed back once it has slipped through your hands. It can, however, be recovered or made up if it has been spent foolishly by doing more in the same or less time than is usually done. Like money, time—or at least what is done in the context of time—can be managed. Learning to do so *takes* time, of course, but it is an investment that can pay large dividends. Finally, time, like money, is cumulative. If you save a few minutes each hour of the day, it can add up at the end to a sizeable amount. This leads to our second assumption.

2. Time *is* money. It is a resource more precious than gold and is available to everyone in equal shares. It is our basic currency in education. It is the only resource that can be converted directly into student learning. You are wealthy or poor in this resource depending on how skilled or unskilled you are in managing your time.

Scheduling and Managing Instructional Time

There are two major elements involved in managing instructional time—scheduling activities (allocated time) and sticking to one's schedule (actual time). For most people, the former comes easily; for many, the latter is nearly impossible. The purpose of this section is to provide you with some guidelines which, hopefully, will make both tasks easier and help you reach the instructional goals you have set for your students.

Allocated Time

There are three levels of allocated time: (1) the amount of time the students are in school (school time), (2) the amount of time they are in your classroom (class time), and (3) the amount of time in which you and they are engaged in instructional activities (instructional time). Your current schedule probably reflects all three levels.

The amount of time the students are in school depends on individual school board policies regarding the length of the school day for students of different ages, the starting and stopping times that the district administration sets for your building, and such factors as student absence and tardiness, excused absences such as visits to the doctor or dentist, trips or class parties, and nonexcused absences such as playing "hooky." School time can be determined—for any given reporting period, for example—by figuring the length of time in one school day, multiplying by the number of school days in the reporting period, and subtracting time for any incidents of absence or tardiness that occurred during the time being considered.

The amount of time students are in class depends largely on the length of their lunch break and on the number and lengths of their recess periods. To determine class time, subtract lunch and recess time from the length of the school day.

The amount of time students spend in instruction depends on what other activities occur in the classroom. "Organizational" activities, such as those listed in Table 6.1, account for much of the noninstructional time. These activities often must be taken care of before any instruction can take place, or they are events that interrupt instruction. However, we are not recommending that organizational activities be eliminated (although some of them, perhaps, can be), but that you minimize the amount of time you spend on them, since they compete with instructional activities for valuable time. Instructional time is also reduced by interruptions either from events in the classroom or from outside sources (other teachers or students, the principal, the intercom, parents, visitors). Again, our point is not that you should eliminate these interruptions, but that you should manage them.

Table 6.1

Organizational Time

Time spent in the classroom on activities
not *directly* related to instruction

Examples

Opening activities	Sharpening pencils
Lunch count/Lunch money	"Rest time" (heads down)
Milk count/Milk money	Clean-up time (room)
Collections for other events	Clean out desks
Flag salute	Put on coats and line
Announcements	up at the door
Special permission slips	Story time
Going to the bathroom	Show and tell
Washing hands	TV programs
Brushing teeth	Calendar/Weather
Getting drinks	

All of these variables—length of school day, absence, tardiness, lunch and recess periods, organizational time, interruptions—affect the amount of time you have to teach your students. In effect, instructional time is whatever you have left over after taking care of all the other activities—not an optimistic picture. However, it underscores the importance of carefully managing your schedule and your time, and of minimizing factors that compete for this time, so that you can be successful at your primary task: teaching the students.

Once you have established how much instructional time you have, your goal is to choose those activities that will help you make the most of the time available, to allocate time to these various activities according to their relative importance (this might be different for different students), and to sequence the activities in a logical and efficient manner.

Actual Time

Despite your best efforts to maximize instructional time, minimize factors that compete for available time, and devise a schedule that reflects instructional priorities, there is still another variable to consider. It is, in fact, perhaps the most important of all time-related variables: *actual time*, or the way in which time is *actually* used, regardless of your plans or intentions. There are several variables that affect actual time.

First, we must consider the times at which your scheduled activities actually start and stop. Does a 10:30 activity start at 10:30? Or does it start at 10:31, 10:33, or 10:35? If these deviations from the schedule occur regularly, the effects will accumulate over time. A recurring 6-minute deviation, for example, becomes half an hour in a week and 2 hours over the course of a month. The starting time for one activity also depends, in part, on the stopping time of the previous activity. Going beyond a scheduled stopping time isn't necessarily bad; it might even be good if it means that an academic task is being given additional time while a nonacademic task is being shortened. However, you will need to recognize that getting off schedule in one activity will unavoidably affect subsequent activities, perhaps throughout the rest of the day.

Second, transition times—the time required to change from one activity to another within the schedule—affect actual instructional time. If you manage transitions effectively, they will not reduce your teaching time to any great extent. But if they are unmanaged, they may take up surprising amounts of time over the course of a day.

Third, students' time on-task affects time use in the classroom. For example, if you allot 10 minutes for a lesson and several students gaze out the window or stare blankly at their desks for 5 of those 10 minutes, your effective teaching time is actually only 5 minutes for these students.

Your effectiveness as a teacher is determined in large part by students' attention to you while you are teaching. Their attentiveness is, in turn, determined largely by how actively you manage their attention.

Fourth, how actively students are required to respond to the material you present affects the quality of your instructional time. If you simply lecture to them, you may see some of the students' attention wander. But if you frequently intersperse your information with questions or tasks to which the students must respond, you increase the effectiveness of your instructional time.

Fifth, the more you can tailor the tasks and materials to students' current abilities, the higher the quality of your instructional time. If the material is too easy, too hard, or not sufficiently interesting, students will begin drifting off-task or become disruptive, and part of your instructional effort will be lost. But if the match between materials or tasks and abilities and interests is a close one, you will maximize the impact of your teaching.

Last, the way you deal with interruptions will, in part, determine your effectiveness. If you tolerate interruptions, you will lose an enormous amount of teaching time over the course of even a single day. But if you actively manage interruptions that threaten to distract students' attention from your presentation, you will have more time to teach, and you will improve the quality of your instructional time.

Why Be Concerned about Managing Time in the Classroom?

The relationship between time use in school and students' learning appears to be very strong (see "A Survey of Research" at the end of Chapter 1 for a brief summary). If you are to give your students every possible chance to succeed in school (and give yourself every chance to succeed as a teacher), you must make the most of every minute in the classroom and make as many minutes available as possible.

Allocated time can be best managed by logically and carefully planning your schedule before the first day of school in the fall—or before the first day that you implement these procedures—then revising the schedule as necessary. Actual time can be managed only by carefully monitoring it throughout the day. Although this sounds as if it will increase your level of stress, the opposite is true. Planning your time carefully and being prepared to deal with interruptions and to make up for lost time will help you develop the necessary skills and composure to handle almost any day.

Who Is Involved in Managing Time?

The teacher is, in effect, the "manager" of the classroom, with primary responsibility for managing instructional time. Aides or volunteers, if they are available, can also play valuable roles in the time management process. However, their effectiveness in helping you reach your goals for the students will depend in large part on how wisely you use their time (see Chapter 3 for guidelines on using others' time effectively).

Parents also play a critical role in effective management of instructional time. They are responsible for seeing that their children go to school each day and arrive for class on time. Many schoolchildren are capable of handling these responsibilities themselves, and they should be expected to do so. However, it is the parents who can be held legally responsible if a child is declared truant. For this reason, parents can be seen as potential intervention agents if a student is habitually late or absent from class.

Finally, students—even though they are minors—are not innocent bystanders to all that happens to them. They can and should be given the responsibility—and be *held* responsible—for giving themselves every opportunity to succeed in school. They can do so by coming to school regularly, by being on time, by obeying classroom and school rules, by paying attention to their work, by completing their assignments, and by giving their best effort in all they do at school. Not all students will be motivated to do these things for themselves. Indeed, not all students will know how to carry out these responsibilities successfully. But all students should hear this message in school—that adults have high expectations of them and that adults will be most willing to help them reach these expectations if the students recognize that they are partners in the process and not merely spectators to it.

How to Manage Instructional Time

Learning how to manage your instructional time may seem a formidable task at first. However, like any task, it can be broken down into simpler steps. Read over this section and the following section, "Analyzing Your Current Schedule," once or twice before you start looking at your own schedule. We believe that as you work through the material, you will begin to see your time as a tangible resource that can be allocated according to your instructional objectives and priorities.

Managing Allocated Time

First, as suggested in the report of the National Commission on Excellence in Education (1983), learn to maximize school time, class time, and instructional time for your students. You might feel that you have little control over school time or instructional time in your building, and this may be true. However, you can remind others, whenever they suggest actions that would reduce students' instructional time, that student learning will suffer as a consequence. Even if you do not have the power or the inclination to lengthen the school day or the school year, you can work with your building or district administrative staff on policies that protect instructional time (e.g., those affecting lunch or recess breaks) or on programs designed to increase attendance rates, decrease tardiness, or decrease unexcused absences. Many of the same strategies described in this book for promoting good student behavior in school (e.g., use of incentive systems, competition, or public posting of feedback on important variables) can be used on a larger scale to address problems of excessive absence, tardiness, or unexcused leaves such as being out of class without a pass, "skipping" all or part of a school day, and so on.

You can also preserve instructional time by minimizing the time spent on organizational activities (see Table 6.1) and on interruptions. Try to eliminate any organizational activity that is not essential or does not contribute to your instructional goals. If the activity is necessary, streamline it as much as possible. You may want to teach students how to perform some of the organizational tasks, holding them to a firm time schedule. For example, if coming in from recess and getting back to work is chaotic and time-consuming, show students how to do this activity quickly and quietly, then have them practice it until their performance is satisfactory. This might take a half hour or more, but the time is well invested. If you show them the right way initially, you are not likely to have problems with this task again.

To manage interruptions, try posting a sign on the outside of your door saying something like "Our time is short; we're busy trying to stretch it. Please leave a note or catch me outside of class." You might even want to have a note pad and pencil available for would-be interrupters to use. You won't eliminate all interruptions this way, but you will cut down on a number of them. Initially, your colleagues might wonder what is going on in your room that's so important. After a time, they will realize that "what's so important" is giving students a chance to learn. They'll soon leave you alone until your break time. If you take the initiative to get back to them quickly after receiving a note, they'll learn to respect your system as effective and efficient. When interruptions *do* occur, you might ask the person, "Is it an emergency, or can it wait?" Answering this question will help others judge whether they really need to interrupt you during your class time.

Second, select activities with the greatest teaching potential. Teachers are often tempted by activities that they think will be fun for students, or that will occasionally "give the kids a break" from instruction. While school should be fun, it should also be productive: it must have content the students can actually use. Many activities are justified because they supposedly "foster social interaction," "enhance creativity," or "promote independence." While such goals are praiseworthy, it is questionable how many activities in a weekly class schedule actually help students meet these objectives. While teachers may feel such activities *should* help students reach those goals, there is no hard evidence that they do unless you teach to those goals directly (as for reading and arithmetic) and objectively measure the results. Thus, a field trip is a good use of time *if* you thoroughly prepare students for it, carefully structure the activity, and hold the students accountable for certain skills and information upon their return—and if there is no more efficient way to accomplish the same goals. If students are not prepared for what they will see or do, are out of control on the bus or at the destination, and cannot tell you what they have learned when they return, then the field trip is not a productive use of available learning time.

Third, allocate time to various selected activities on the basis of their importance. Does the time you spend on a particular activity reflect its relative worth? In one time analysis study we conducted, we found tremendous differences—even between different classrooms at the same grade level—in the distribution of time across activities. One teacher spent 60% of the available instructional time on reading and other language arts activities and a minimum amount of time on organizational or noninstructional events. Another teacher at the same grade level spent only 25% of the time on reading and language arts and almost as much on organizational tasks. Although both teachers probably would say reading instruction is one of the most important activities in the primary grades, their schedules reflected different priorities. Remember, too, that a look at *actual* time use would likely reveal even more disparity between the two classrooms. Not surprisingly, the first teacher's students had much better reading scores than did the second teacher's students.

There are at least three criteria that can be used to determine how available time should be allocated to various activities. One criterion is simply to use your best judgment—to schedule what you think will be necessary to cover the material. This is probably the weakest criterion since, as we have already seen, different teachers have different perspectives on the matter. Also, it is oriented too much toward the *process* of teaching rather than its *results* (i.e., "How long will it take me to cover this material?" versus "How long will it take the students to learn it?").

The second criterion consists of the guidelines made available in many states by the Department of Education for balancing school curricula. In Oregon, for example, the State Department of Education recommends certain percentage allocations of time to subject areas, as shown in Table 6.2. Notice that these recommendations change slightly from primary to intermediate grades.

Table 6.2
Suggested K-8 Curriculum Balance

Instructional Program*	Primary K-3	Intermediate 4-6
Art Education	7%	7%
Health Education	7%	8%
Language Arts	40%	35%
Mathematics	15%	15%
Music Education	7%	7%
Physical Education	8%	8%
Science	7%	10%
Social Studies	9%	10%

*Areas of study such as traffic safety education, career education, environmental education, consumer education, ethics and morality education, and citizenship education may be combined in curriculum where most appropriate.

Source: Oregon Department of Education. *Elementary-secondary guide for Oregon schools: Planning for standard implementation.* Salem, Oreg.: Author, 1980.

These guidelines are also weak in their *a priori* determination of what is appropriate and in their assumption that all students need the same amount of instruction in all curriculum areas.

A third approach is to allocate time to subjects *for groups of students* on the basis of their abilities and performance. If some students are having difficulty in reading, for example, you can allocate more time to reading instruction for that group. If some are experiencing trouble learning math, they can receive more math time. In such a system, allocations might be done weekly or monthly and revised as necessary. Obviously, this procedure would also require considerable coordination of various schedules. This can be done by laying all the information out on one chart.

Figure 6.1 illustrates one of many possible schedules for a morning in an elementary classroom. The class is divided into three groups. Group A consists of 8 to 10 of the highest performing students; Group B, 6 to 8 of the most average students; and Group C, 4 to 6 of the lowest students. Notice that most instruction is provided in small groups. Considerable use is also made of peer-tutoring and volunteers. This schedule allows all basic skill instruction to be provided before lunch. The afternoon can be used for health/science/social studies, art and music, and physical education. Instruction in each of these areas can be provided 2 or 3 days per week. Time is also allocated each afternoon for completion of seatwork, criterion or "catchup" teaching time (see the discussion following), and other academically related tasks at the teacher's discretion. The section

Figure 6.1
Sample Time Allocation Chart

	Reading	Math	Spelling	Writing	Seatwork/ Free Reading	Health/Science/ Social Studies	Art/Music	P.E./Recess
8:10					A & B	C		
8:20				All groups				
8:30								
8:40						A & B Enrichment		
8:50	C		A & B (w/tutors)					
9:00				A & B Journals				
9:10								
9:20				A tutors C				
9:30	B							
9:40								
9:50	A	D & C (w/tutors)						
10:00								
10:10		C			A & B			
10:20								
10:30								
10:40	C (w/tutors)	A & B						
10:50								All groups
11:00			C	A & B Journals				
11:10								
11:20			All groups					
11:30	A tutors B		C					
Group A	20 min.	20 min.	20 min.	30 min.	40 min.	enrichment	in p.m.	10 min.
Group B	40 min.	40 min.	20 min.	30 min.	40 min.	enrichment	in p.m.	10 min.
Group C	60 min.	50 min.	30 min.	40 min.	in p.m.	10 min.	in p.m.	10 min.

A: High Group

B. Middle Group

C: Low Group

	Total Instruc- tional Time	Total Teacher Time
Group A	130 min.	60 min.
Group B	170 min.	70 min.
Group C	190 min.	120 min.

at the bottom of the table indicates the number of minutes of instructional and practice time each group receives in each area every day. It also notes how much time the teacher spends directly with each of the groups.

Notice that in this arrangement the teacher spends much of the time with students who require the most instruction. Thus, the lowest performing students receive almost 50% more academic instruction time than the highest achievers. This type of schedule gives all students a chance to experience success in the classroom.

Two other points must be made about scheduling time on the basis of students' needs. First, you can schedule additional academic time beyond regular instructional time by inserting into the master schedule an event each afternoon called "criterion teaching time." During this period, you and your aides or volunteers, if available, can tutor students individually or in small groups to help them master skills they find troublesome. You might repeat or preview difficult lessons with students or bring them up to criterion performance on particular tasks or skills they have had trouble mastering.

A secondary strategy for helping students reach mastery on new or troublesome tasks is to schedule several brief "distributed practice times" each day. If students can practice skills at various times throughout the day—perhaps in different locations with different tutors—they will master the skills more quickly and be able to apply them more broadly than if they were taught the skills only by one teacher at one time and place. Set aside blocks of time for practice sessions each day. They can be as little as 10 or even 5 minutes. The material practiced should review the concepts students had trouble with during the regular lessons. Classroom aides, tutors, or volunteers also can help run the distributed practice sessions, freeing you for other instructional activities.

Finally, arrange the selected activities in a logical sequence. We have many notions in education about student performance across the school day. We hear that students work best in the morning and are "burned out" in the afternoon; that they work poorly in the morning if they have not had a good breakfast; and that young minds tend to wander, so we can't expect too much of them at one time. While there is no doubt some truth to these admonitions, many of the variables, such as whether a child has had breakfast, a good night's sleep, and the like, are out of your control as a teacher. But you do have control over at least two variables. First, you can schedule the most important activities of the day at times when most of the students are likely to be at their peak levels of functioning; and second, you can structure other periods to compensate for slightly lower levels of alertness by using extra praise, more required student participation, and so on. Thus, reading probably should be taught in the morning, with criterion teaching time for reading in the afternoon and distributed practice on new or difficult reading skills throughout the day.

Another way to gain the greatest benefit from instructional activities is to schedule an activity that students particularly like immediately after one that is less preferred. If the preferred activity is made available *only* if students meet some specified performance criterion on the first activity, the second task is likely to act as a reward for the first and to strengthen students' performance.

Managing Actual Time

First, make sure you manage the starting and stopping of all planned activities. An activity's start time depends on the stop time of the previous activity. You can best manage the start and stop times if you allow 1 or 2 minutes between activities for students to make the transition to the next activity. You can also use this time to answer their questions, assist those who need help, mark points on a feedback chart (discussed in Chapter 11), and praise students who have been working well.

Stop times can be monitored by setting a standard kitchen timer at the beginning of an activity. Some teachers prefer to set the timer for 3 or 5 minutes *less* than the amount of time remaining. When the timer rings, it is not a signal to start the next event (which might produce panic), but a reminder to finish up the present activity. When teachers have time to finish one task and make the transition to the next one, they tend to feel in better control of their classroom time and activities. If you find that you cannot finish an activity in the 3 to 5 minutes remaining after the timer rings, you might choose to use your scheduled criterion teaching time to do so in the afternoon. If this problem occurs frequently, you will know that you need to speed up your instructional pace, increase the time you allocate to that activity, or somehow squeeze the scheduled lessons into the time available.

Second, manage transition times carefully. These periods tend to be less structured than instructional times. Once a lesson ends, the students often feel that the classroom structure has been relaxed, and they may become more disruptive. You can control this tendency by managing the time between scheduled activities, as described in the transition time section of this chapter.

Third, manage students' time on-task by using praise (Chapter 4) and other incentive procedures such as point systems (Chapter 11), timings (this chapter), and game-like task structures (this chapter).

Fourth, give students frequent opportunities to respond during instructional times. Research indicates that responding actively increases students' attention to their tasks and enhances their learning. For this reason, we suggest that you encourage students to respond frequently during your lessons. While question-and-answer, discussion, or project formats are traditional methods of involving students, the most efficient way seems to be the use of choral or unison responses by all the students to questions you ask or task directions you give. One problem with traditional instructional formats is that each student has only a few opportunities to participate during each lesson. Also, the students who respond the most are usually the students who already know the most. Students who need to be involved in the give and take of classroom participation seldom speak out. However, if all students must respond to each question or task direction, every student receives the greatest number of opportunities to practice and be given feedback on the new information or the new skills.

Fifth, match students' materials and assignments to their abilities and skill levels. To the extent possible, individualize lessons and assignments so that each student is working on material at an appropriate level of difficulty. Ideally, each student would have different materials and/or assignments. In practice, however, it would be extremely difficult to supervise and manage individual assignments for 20, 25, or 30 students. Thus a practical alternative is to use ability grouping. Divide students into three instructional groups for reading and, if at all possible, for arithmetic (more groups make scheduling impracticable). Grouping should be done on the basis of students' pre-test performances. Regrouping can be done periodically to accommodate varying rates of student progress. However, this step often can be avoided if criterion teaching time and distributed practice time are used well. The lowest performing group should be allotted more instructional time than students who learn more quickly.

Sixth, manage disruptions that occur during your planned activities. Disruptions can be caused by students in your room or by outsiders who interrupt while you are teaching. Students who disrupt the class usually can be managed with praise and points when they are behaving appropriately (see Chapters 4 and 11) and with the warning and loss of privileges procedure when misbehaving (see Chapter 10). Some teachers keep track of the amount of time lost when these students act up and have them "repay" the same amount of time during recess or after school. Outside interruptors can be handled in the manner described earlier under the topic of maximizing instructional time.

If you follow the guidelines suggested in this chapter for managing time and activities in your classroom, you will soon begin to experience the results—a more efficient, orderly classroom; students who pay better attention, are less disruptive, and achieve more; and the satisfaction of being in control and of achieving greater effectiveness as a teacher.

Analyzing Your Current Schedule

To help you examine how you are currently using the instructional time available in your school day, we have devised a schedule analysis procedure. To do the analysis, start by reviewing your current written schedule or by constructing a schedule on a form similar to Figure 6.2. The more detail you include, the easier the schedule will be to analyze. You may even put in transition times if they appear in your schedule. When the schedule is complete, turn to Figure 6.3, the Schedule Analysis form, and follow these steps.

1. Compute the number of minutes in your school week. To do so, determine the number of hours and minutes in each school day (number of complete hours x 60 minutes per hour + number of extra minutes beyond the last full hour) and multiply by 5 (since there are typically 5 school days in each week). Enter this number, which probably will fall somewhere between 1,600 and 2,400 minutes, in the Min/Week space at the top of the form and on the blank next to (ST) (for school time) near the middle of the page.

2. From your schedule, determine the number of minutes for each activity, and enter that figure in the TIME column, next to the appropriate curriculum area. Then determine the number of times each week that the activity occurs for that length of time and enter this number in the DAYS/WEEK column. Sometimes you will have more than one entry for a given curriculum area, particularly in the areas of Language Arts/Library, Organizational, and Lunch/Recess. For example, the area Language Arts/Library might include reading, writing, spelling, story time, library visits, or other activities. You might want to modify the form to include each of the various language arts activities you provide for your students. As an alternative, you can squeeze several entries onto a line:

AREA	TIME	DAYS/WEEK	MIN/WEEK
	60	5 ⎫	300 ⎫
	20	5 ⎬	100 ⎬ 470
Language	20	2 ⎭	40 ⎭
Arts/Library	30	1	30

3. When you have gone through the entire schedule and entered all scheduled activities onto the form, multiply the number of minutes an activity lasts by the number of times it takes place each week. If you have more than one entry for a subject area, multiply the duration (minutes) by the frequency (number of times) for each of the entries, then add the answers together to determine how many minutes are being scheduled each week for that curriculum area. Enter the number for each line in the MIN/WEEK column.

Figure 6.2
Weekly Schedule

	Time Spent on Activity	Mon.	Tues.	Wed.	Thurs.	Fri.
8:00						
8:30						
9:00						
9:30						
10:00						
10:30						
11:00						
11:30						
12:00						
12:30						
1:00						
1:30						
2:00						
2:30						
3:00						
3:30						
4:00						

Figure 6.3
Schedule Analysis

School _____ Min/Week _____ Grade _____

AREA	TIME	DAYS/ WEEK	MIN/ WEEK	%	RANK	ACHIEVE. SCORE
Language Arts/Library	_____	_____	_____	___	_____	_____
Math	_____	_____	_____	___	_____	_____
Social Studies	_____	_____	_____	___	_____	_____
Science	_____	_____	_____	___	_____	_____
Health	_____	_____	_____	___	_____	_____
Physical Education	_____	_____	_____	___	_____	_____
Art	_____	_____	_____	___	_____	_____
Music	_____	_____	_____	___	_____	_____
Organizational	_____	_____	_____	___	_____	_____
Lunch/Recess	_____	_____	_____	___	_____	_____
Total			_____ (ST)	_____/100		
			_____ (CT)			
			_____ (IT)			

Comments/Recommendations

_____

_____

_____

_____

_____

_____

_____

_____

_____

4. Subtract the number for Lunch/Recess in the MIN/WEEK column from the total school time (ST) and enter it in the space marked (CT) (for class time). This figure is the amount of time students spend in your classroom each week.

5. Subtract the number for Organizational in the MIN/WEEK column from the (CT) figure and enter it into the space marked (IT) (for instructional time). This is the amount of time you have available for teaching your students each week.

6. Next, divide each of the figures in the MIN/WEEK column by the amount of class time you have each week—the figure in the (CT) space in the middle of the page. Enter these percentages in the % column. These are the percentages of available class time you devote to each of the activities on your schedule.

7. Rank each of the activity areas by assigning the number "1" to the highest percentage, "2" to the next highest, and so on until you have a rank number for each of the lines. These rankings indicate your priorities for time use, as reflected by your schedule.

8. Finally, if you want to do so and have the information, enter the subject area achievement test scores for your class in the ACHIEVE. SCORE column opposite the respective curriculum areas. There will not be a score for each area, but there should be scores for each of the major academic subjects (i.e., reading, math, and possibly science and social studies). You can use these scores to evaluate whether students' achievement levels are satisfactory within each area and whether there is a relationship between their scores and the time you allocate to various areas. For example, if their math scores seem to be lower than you would like, look at the time you allocate for math instruction. Does it seem sufficient to help students improve their scores next time they are tested? If not, perhaps you can use this analysis to find ways of increasing this time allocation.

The space that reads ____/100, near the right center of the page, is simply an accuracy check. The percentages listed in the % column should total 100%. If they do not, recheck your figures, starting back with the entries on the form taken from your schedule. This step usually uncovers any errors made in the analysis process. The bottom part of the form can be used for notes on what you have learned by doing the analysis and what you want to change, if anything, as a result.

Scheduling and Managing Instructional Time
Implementation Checklist

1. Does your current schedule minimize organizational time and maximize instructional time?
2. Are the instructional activities on your schedule efficient? That is, will they help students learn what you want them to learn?
3. Does the time you allocate to chosen activities reflect students' instructional needs?
4. Are the chosen activities arranged to give you the greatest possible control over manageable variables that might affect student learning and to give students the greatest possible chance of succeeding in school?
5. Are you successfully managing the times at which you start and stop planned activities?
6. Are you successfully managing transition times?
7. Are you successfully using praise and other motivational activities to manage students' time on-task?
8. Are you giving students frequent opportunities to respond during the tasks and activities you provide for them?
9. Are you doing everything you can to ensure that all students are working on materials appropriate to their abilities and skill levels?
10. Are you using procedures to minimize outside interruptions and in-class disruptions, and are these procedures working as well as you would like them to?
11. Have you analyzed your schedule recently to determine whether your current time allocations match students' present instructional needs?

Managing Transition Time

Transition time is the time it takes to change from one activity to another. Transition time can occur when:

- Students remain at their seats and change from one subject to another.
- Students move from their seats to an activity in another part of the classroom.
- Students move from somewhere else in the classroom back to their seats.
- Students leave the classroom to go outside or to another part of the school building.
- Students come back into the classroom from outside or another part of the building.

Why Teach Transition Time?

There are several important reasons to teach transition time. First, it minimizes the amount of nonacademic time that children spend in school. Second, it provides teachers with more time for academic instruction. Third, it decreases the number of behavior problems that often occur during this unstructured time.

Observations in typical elementary school classrooms indicate that a class commonly spends from 5 to 10 minutes changing from one activity or place to another. An average class could change activities approximately 10 times a day. If they spent 8 minutes for each transition time, that would mean a loss of 80 minutes a day for instruction. This figure represents 20% of a school day, or the equivalent of one entire day each week spent on transition time alone. One teacher who used the following procedures in his third and fourth grade classes spent only about 30 seconds for each transition time. This amounted to a time savings of more than an hour a day.

Who Is Involved in Transition Time?

Transition time involves the teacher as well as the students. The students' role is simply to follow the rules for a quick and quiet transition time. The teacher's role in transition time is to be prepared for each subject and monitor student behavior during this time.

It is important that all the materials for each lesson during the day be prepared before school begins in the morning and placed in the room where they are to be used. This saves valuable time since the teacher doesn't have to rummage through files, run to the ditto machine, or leave a group of students to search for a missing book. Many teachers have found that they have more time for instruction and that teaching is easier when all the materials for the entire day are prepared and organized by group or subject at the beginning of the day. Aides, volunteers, and students can help with various aspects of preparation.

Another important reason for advanced preparation is that it enables the teacher or aide to monitor the students' behavior during transition time. Either the teacher or the aide should watch the students while transition time is taking place and give specific praise to students who are following the rules. An example of a specific praise statement in this situation would be "Sue, you didn't talk at all during transition time. That's terrific!" How much to praise and when is discussed in the following section.

How to Teach Transition Time

Transition time needs to be quick and quiet so that it doesn't interrupt the flow of academic activities. There are four rules for a quick and quiet transition time, which should be posted on a chart.

1. Move quietly.
2. Put your books away and get what you need for the next activity. (You may need to state what that activity will be and what materials students need for it.)
3. Move your chairs quietly. (In some classes with small-group instruction, students carry their desk chairs to the group for seating there.)
4. Keep your hands and feet to yourself.

Introduce transition time to the students by using the following script. Use it at the beginning of the first transition time of the day you teach the procedure. You should schedule 15 to 20 minutes for the introduction. After it is introduced and the children have practiced it, only a few seconds will be needed for review later on. A shortened version of the script is included for review.

Script for Introducing Transition Time

Teacher	Students
"Transition time is the time it takes to change what you are doing. What is transition time?" (Point to the chart.) (signal)	"The time it takes to change what you are doing."
"It is important that transition time be quick and quiet. What is important about transition time?" (signal)	"That it be quick and quiet."
"That's right. I'm going to tell you some ways for transition time to be quick and quiet."	

Teacher	Students
"Move quietly during transition time. What is one way for transition time to be quick and quiet?" (signal)	"Move quietly."
"Good! That's one way for transition time to be quick and quiet. Now I'm going to tell you some more ways."	
"Put books away and get what you need for the next activity. What's another way to make transition time be quick and quiet?" (signal)	"Put books away and get what you need for the next activity."
"Now I'll tell you another way. Move chairs quietly. What is another way for transition time to be quick and quiet?" (signal)	"Move chairs quietly."
"Terrific. Here's the last way for transition time to be quick and quiet. Keep your hands and feet to yourself. What's the last way to make transition time quick and quiet?" (signal)	"Keep your hands and feet to yourself."
"That's right. Let's say all four ways to make transition time quick and quiet." (Point to the chart.) (signal)	"Move quietly. Put books away and get what you need for the next activity. Move chairs quietly. Keep your hands and feet to yourself."
"I'm going to show you what I mean. This is what I do to change activities at my desk." (Teacher sits at the desk. Puts one book away. Gets another book out. Has a pencil ready. Sits quietly and waits.)	
"What did I do during this transition time?" (Call on individual students.)	"Moved quietly." "Put book away and got what you needed for the next activity."
"Good. You're really watching. Now watch again while I show you a different kind of transition time." (Teacher puts the book away. Gets another book and pencil. Stands up and pushes the chair in quietly. Walks to another table. Sits down. Opens the book. Waits quietly.)	

Teacher	Students
"What did I do during this transition time?" (Call on individual students.)	"Moved quietly." "Put book away and got what you needed for the next activity." "Moved chair quietly." "Kept hands and feet to yourself."
"It's important to know all these ways to make transition time quick and quiet. It's even more important to actually do these things during transition time."	
"I'm going to watch. I know you can change what you're doing by moving quietly, getting the proper materials ready, moving your chairs quietly, and keeping your hands and feet to yourself."	

The teacher should signal a transition time by simply saying: "It's transition time. Get ready for _____. You need _____." The students need to be held accountable for following the four rules discussed. If students do not follow all four rules, they must go back to their seats and do it again. This is similar to holding a firm criterion when teaching reading or any other skill. Repeating the process might involve individual students if only a few do it incorrectly or the whole class if a majority of the students do not follow the rules. Although this practice will require some extra time at first, it should pay dividends shortly as students learn that you are serious about safeguarding instructional time in the classroom.

As an added incentive to help your students learn the importance of rapid, orderly transitions, you can time them with a stopwatch or other device and tell them how long the transitions take. If you set a criterion for them or challenge them to be faster, but still quiet, chances are you will get good transitions very quickly.

Because transition time involves relatively little structure, the teacher will need to use praise more often than during work times. The praise should be specific and should name the student and the rule that was correctly followed: "David, you're really keeping your hands and feet to yourself." When quick and quiet transitions become routine, the amount of praise delivered to students can be decreased.

On the day you introduce transition time, briefly review the rules with the students before each transition time and increase your praise for rule following. Use the following script to review transition time the day after you introduce it.

Script for Reviewing Transition Time

Teacher	Students
"I want to see what you remember about transition time."	
"What is important about transition time?" (signal)	"That it be quick and quiet."
(If students don't remember, model the answer, then ask the question again.)	
"That's right. Transition time needs to be quick and quiet."	
"What's one way to make transition time quick and quiet?" (Call on individual students.)	(Students should answer by stating any of the four rules.) "Move quietly."
"What's another?"	"Put books away and get what you need for the next activity."
"What's another way?"	"Move chairs quietly."
"What's the last way?"	"Keep hands and feet to yourself."
"Good! You know all the rules for transition time. I'll be watching today to see who knows how to follow them."	

Review the rules once by repeating them to the students and once by asking individual students to tell what they are. On successive days, a review of the rules is needed only if students are not following them. The review script may also be used to review after the students have been away from school for a holiday, vacation, or long weekend.

After you have taught transition time to your class, you should have more time available for instruction and fewer behavior problems during transitions. Transition time is simple to teach to students and makes the entire school day more pleasant and productive.

Managing Transition Time
Implementation Checklist

1. Are all materials ready for each subject and activity?
2. Are these materials organized so they are easily accessible?
3. Are all students' materials ready for each subject and activity?
4. Have you reviewed the rules for transition time with the students recently?
5. Are you or your aide watching students during transition time to be sure they follow the four rules?
6. Are you or your aide giving specific praise to those who follow the rules?
7. Are you marking the feedback chart (discussed in Chapter 11)?

Using Timings and Time Limits

Timings and time limits are two ways of using time to manage student behavior. *Timings* require the use of a stopwatch, timer, or some other device to determine the length of an activity or particular behavior or to keep track of a predetermined amount of time. They can be used to time the transition periods between activities or to provide proficiency practice in such skills as reading, recalling math facts, or reciting other information that students are expected to master.

Time limits involve giving students predetermined amounts of time to work on some assigned task. Although time limits are implicit in any classroom schedule, they can be used to motivate students when you announce them or shorten the limit to challenge students or urge them to greater efforts.

Why Use Timings and Time Limits?

Timings and time limits can have tremendous incentive value for students, especially when they are coupled with feedback or with contests in which the students compete with each other, with their own best scores, or against some criterion in a challenging, game-like event. Timings and time limits are simple, easy, and inexpensive procedures that help students move from a preoccupation with accuracy ("I must be correct on each of the problems I attempt, even if it means only getting a few problems done") to a proficiency outlook ("I must be correct most of the time, but I must also try to get as many problems done as possible"). Encouraging students to increase their accuracy *rates*—and not just their accuracy—also helps both teacher and students to use the time available most productively.

When to Use Timings and Time Limits

Timings and time limits can be considered appropriate incentives whenever a student or group of students has reached an initial accuracy criterion (i.e., 70 to 80% correct) on new skills you have been teaching. You can then begin shifting your incentives from students' accuracy to their rates of task or unit completion. Also, when students are already operating on a rate criterion but are not using their time well, you might consider employing timings or time limits to bring them back to their former rates of task completion. This method reminds them that they can do better and that you continue to expect high levels of performance from them, even though they have not shown those levels recently. It is one more way to communicate high expectations to your students and to get better performances from them.

Who Is Involved in Using Timings and Time Limits?

Teachers—and their designated helpers—and students have roles to play in the use of timings and time limits. Teachers, and their assistants, conduct the timings and provide instructions, reminders, feedback, praise, and corrective instruction. The students' role is to beat the clock, the competition, or their own previous best scores.

How to Use Timings and Time Limits

When you first begin to use timings or time limits with your students, be sure to introduce the procedures to them. You can use either the script provided in this book or your own words to describe what will happen and what is expected of the students.

Script for Introducing Timings and Time Limits

Teacher	Students
"Today I would like to start something new with you. It is called a timing. You might have done it in one of your other classes."	
"Timings are fun. They're like a game or a contest. The goal is to see how much *good* work you can get done in the amount of time I give you. Good work is work that is correct and neat. Sometimes we'll play the game in other ways, but mostly we will play it to see how much *good* work you can do in the time I give you. What is the goal of timings?" (signal)	"To see how much *good* work we can get done in the time you give us."
(If the students respond by saying, "how much work we can get done," correct them by saying, "Not just how much *work*, but how much *good* work. It has to be good or it doesn't count." You will need to tell them what you mean by "good work.")	
"That's right. To see how much good work you can get done in the time I give you."	
"When we have a timing, I will give you some work to do. Then I will say, 'This is a timing.' What will I say?" (signal)	"This is a timing."
"Good. It will always be work that you know how to do."	

Teacher	Students
"Then I will remind you of the goal of the timing and tell you to get ready. When I say, 'Get ready,' put your pencil up, like this." (Demonstrate by holding your pencil just above your assignment paper.) "What do you do when I say, 'Get ready'?" (signal)	"Put our pencils up."
"Great. When I say 'Begin,' you should start right away. When I say 'Stop,' you should stop right away and draw a line after the last problem you finished. What do you do when I say 'Stop'?" (signal)	"Stop right away and draw a line where we finished."
"Okay. Then we'll find out how you did and compare scores. I think you'll find that it's fun. Now let's practice."	
Conduct a practice timing, using a task assignment all the students can do. Follow the instructions in this script, and give the students feedback on how well they follow their role.	

Script for Reviewing Timings and Time Limits

Teacher	Students
"Let's review. What's the goal of the timings?"	"To see how much good work we can do in the time you give us."
"Right. What do you do when I say, 'Get ready'?"	"Put our pencils up."
"Yes. When do you stop and what do you do then?"	"Stop right away and draw a line where we finished."
"Okay! You've got it! Let's do a timing now."	

At the beginning of each timing or time limit period, clearly announce to students "This is a timing." They must be aware of the fact if timing is to motivate them to do well. Initially, remind students that the purpose of timing is to see how much "good work" they can get done. "Good work" is defined as work that is accurate and reasonably neat.

Next, start all of the students on the timing at exactly the same moment. By standardizing the procedure, you will be able to compare students' performances over time. It will also help students make better use of the feedback they receive. Since they will likely compare their scores with each other, the comparisons will be fair only if everyone actually starts and stops at the same time. However, while comparisons between students are probably unavoidable, do not let them make too much of this information. Some students will naturally have better timing scores than others. Unless you have structured a competition between students of equal ability, state that comparisons with other students do not mean much. Instead, you might want to encourage students to compare their current scores with their own past scores or to some criterion score you have identified as appropriate for those students. You might want to use different criteria for different groups of students, based on their current ability levels. However, this should be done discreetly to avoid teasing or claims of unfairness.

You can make scores more meaningful as feedback if you have students keep track of their own previous scores on comparable tasks. This can be done in the form of a graph (if the students have been taught—in math class, for example—to construct and interpret graphs) or simply on a list containing dates and scores. You might also want to post a criterion score and/or have students publicly post their scores on a wall chart. To make the best use of this information, you will occasionally need to have students look at the chart or their lists or graphs. Students do not necessarily attach any special meaning to these items unless they are taught to do so. For example, you can draw their attention to this information, by putting everyone's name on the board who has met the criterion or beaten their own previous best score, by giving these names to the principal or having them read over the public address system, or by permitting these students to have some special reinforcing activity at the end of the day or the week.

You should meet individually with the students who do not reach the criterion or beat their own best score to determine how they can do so during the next timing session. If a student fails to "win" at the timing game only occasionally, you should not be overly concerned. But if a child "loses" at the game chronically, you should do whatever you can to help reverse this situation. You can tutor the student (or have someone else do this) to increase the academic response rate, adjust the criterion to be more realistic for the student, or—if the personal best score is unusually high—have the student work to beat the average of all past scores. Once a student begins to experience success at timing, the game is likely to be an effective motivator in the future.

Timings and Time Limits
Implementation Checklist

1. Have you reviewed the procedures for timing with students and reminded them of its goals recently?
2. Do you have the worksheets or other materials you need ready for any timings you plan to conduct today?
3. Have students been starting and stopping at the exact same moment in recent timings? (Remember to monitor for this.)
4. Have you drawn attention to the meaning of students' timing game scores recently? (Remember to do this regularly.)
5. Are materials ready and time scheduled for any reinforcement activities you have planned in conjunction with timings?
6. Are any of your students losing more often than they are winning at timing games? If so, how are you working to reverse this situation?

A Survey of Research

Scheduling

The literature of elementary education contains little empirical advice to guide teachers in constructing classroom schedules. Most of the research in this area has been conducted with handicapped children. This research does show that student achievement in school is closely related to the amount of time spent actively engaged in appropriate academic tasks (e.g., Rosenshine, 1976). This well-documented relationship has several implications for schedule construction, as noted in this chapter.

Orelove (1982) discussed implications of the time-achievement relationship—and of other program goals, such as integration, functional training, and normalization—for devising the classroom schedules of severely handicapped students. Basically, Orelove stated that if we expect our students, regardless of their instructional needs, to meet the goals we set for them, we must design daily schedules that reflect those priorities and adhere to the schedules once they are set.

With respect to nonhandicapped and mildly handicapped students, Paine (1982) studied classroom schedules and actual time use for 55 kindergarten through sixth grade classrooms—all the elementary school classrooms in a district of approximately 2,500 students. He found that (1) considerable differences existed among schools, and among classrooms within schools, in the amount of time made available for academic pursuits; (2) teachers adhered closely to their written schedules; and (3) the amount of time allocated to academic instruction correlated highly with academic achievement in the district. This final point doesn't necessarily mean that performance in all subject areas or for all students was always the highest. It does mean, in part, that where allocated and actual time were high, as in reading, achievement tended to be high; where insufficient time was devoted, as in math, performance tended to fall below desired levels. The findings and recommendations of the National Commission on Excellence in Education (1983) are also highly consistent with the recommendations in this chapter.

Transition Times

Our review of the literature found no published studies that directly addressed the potential problems of transition time between activities. However, we conducted a pilot study from which we learned some important facts about transitions. Kuergeleis, Deutchman, and Paine (1980) measured and intervened in the transition times of a regular fifth grade classroom. Transitions between activities were observed to range up to 20 minutes in length. Since the typical classroom often has a dozen or more transition periods each day, a considerable amount of potential academic time can be lost easily if transitions are not managed. To shorten the transitions in this classroom, the authors introduced a simple timing and feedback procedure. Students were told that they were being timed and were challenged to meet or beat an announced criterion time. They were then clocked with a stopwatch while they made the change from one activity to another. When the last student had completed the transition, the watch was stopped, and the students were told how long the switch had taken them. If the class met or exceeded the criterion, one class member was chosen to take a note to the office to let the principal know of the class's success. Transition times shortened quickly and stayed consistently low—between 30 seconds and 2 minutes. The students never failed to meet the criterion set for them. This procedure was simple but effective.

Timing and Time Limits

Timing has also been reported several times in the literature as an effective procedure for increasing students' academic work rates.

Rainwater and Ayllon (1976) used the timing procedure to increase the reading and math performance of first grade students. The authors found that simply telling the students they were being timed was enough to increase their work rates. However, some feedback or other evidence that timings are taking place and are important probably would be required to maintain this effect. Van Houten and Thompson (1976) used explicit timings to increase the rate at which second graders accurately worked math problems. Two types of timings were employed in this study—a timer was used for the 30-minute math period, and a stopwatch was used for continuous 1-minute segments within the longer period. Not only did students increase their work rates, but they also maintained their initial levels of accuracy. In addition, timing has been used in conjunction with feedback, competition with one's previous scores, and praise as elements of a performance feedback system (Van Houten, Hill, & Parsons, 1975; Van Houten, Morrison, Jarvis, & McDonald, 1974). See the research discussion in Chapter 11 for a description of these procedures.

Two studies have addressed the issue of reducing time limits and the effects that such reductions can have on students' behavior. Ayllon, Garber, and Pisor (1976) evaluated gradual and abrupt reductions in the time given to 10- to 12-year-old mildly retarded students to complete academic work tasks. They found that graduated reductions, from 20 to 15 to 10 to 5 minutes, produced an increase in students' work rates. These improved rates continued when the time was lengthened again to 20 minutes. However, abrupt reductions, from 20 to 5 minutes, produced a *decrease* in work rates *and* brought on emotional side effects. Van Houten and Little (1982) conducted a similar study but obtained quite different results. They evaluated only abrupt reductions in time limits for 14- to 17-year-old mildly retarded students. The abrupt reductions increased the students' rates of accurate responding on math assignments without the emotional side effects observed by Ayllon et al. Math accuracy also improved slightly during the shortened work segments. When 20-minute periods were introduced again, students' work rates decreased.

One explanation Van Houten and Little offered for the divergence between their findings and those of Ayllon et al. is that their intervention was done outside the context of an on-going token economy. The Ayllon et al. students were operating under a token system and might have been upset if they believed that the abrupt reduction in time would prevent them from earning the back-up reinforcers to which they were accustomed. Van Houten and Little's students did not respond emotionally to this shift, perhaps because they had nothing of consequence to lose even if they did not complete their work in the shorter time period. These students were also older by 4 to 5 years. Finally, it is possible, although difficult to determine, that students' reactions to the requirements placed on them in class might be influenced by how the teacher presents those requirements. If the teacher introduces a change by saying, "Well, it's too bad if you don't like it, but that's the way it is," students probably have a different reaction than if the teacher says something like, "You're getting so good at these problems that I'll bet you can do them in even less time than you did before. What do you say—should we try it and see?" This variable can be called anything from sensitivity to "hype," but it is likely to affect how students respond to teachers' directives. For a more thorough explanation of how to make the timing procedure work for you, see Ron Van Houten's book, *Learning Through Feedback* (1980).

References

Ayllon, T., Garber, S., & Pisor, K. Reducing time limits: A means to increase behavior of retardates. *Journal of Applied Behavior Analysis*, 1976, *9*, 247-252.

Kuergeleis, B., Deutchman, L., & Paine, S. *Effects of explicit timings on students' transitions*. Eugene, Oreg.: Direct Instruction Follow Through Project, University of Oregon, 1980.

National Commission on Excellence in Education. *A nation at risk: The imperative for educational reform*. Washington, D.C.: U.S. Department of Education, 1983.

Orelove, F. Developing daily schedules for classrooms of severely handicapped students. *Education and Treatment of Children*, 1982, *5*, 59-68.

Paine, S. *Time, teaching, and student achievement in 55 elementary school classrooms: Data summary and management recommendations*. Eugene, Oreg.: Direct Instruction Follow Through Project, University of Oregon, 1982.

Rainwater, N., & Ayllon, R. Increasing academic performance by using a timer as an antecedent stimulus: A study of four cases. *Behavior Therapy*, 1976, *7*, 672-677.

Rosenshine, B. Classroom instruction. In N. L. Gage (Ed.), *The psychology of teaching methods: Seventy-fifth yearbook of the National Society for the Study of Education.* Chicago: University of Chicago Press, 1976.

Van Houten, R. *Learning through feedback: A systematic approach for improving academic performance.* New York: Human Sciences Press, 1980.

Van Houten, R., Hill, S., & Parsons, M. An analysis of a performance feedback system: The effects of timing and feedback, public posting, and praise upon academic performance and peer interaction. *Journal of Applied Behavior Analysis*, 1975, *8*, 449-457.

Van Houten, R., & Little, G. Increased response rate in special education children following an abrupt reduction in time limit in the absence of a token economy. *Education and Treatment of Children*, 1982, *5*, 23-32.

Van Houten, R., Morrison, E., Jarvis, R., & McDonald, M. The effects of explicit timing and feedback on compositional response rate in elementary school children. *Journal of Applied Behavior Analysis*, 1974, *7*, 547-555.

Van Houten, R., & Thompson, C. The effects of explicit timing on math performance. *Journal of Applied Behavior Analysis*, 1976, *9*, 227-230.

Chapter 7

Managing Materials in the Classroom

Students may often need work materials they do not keep at their desks. These materials might include special pens, books, workbooks, writing paper, ditto pages, and the like which must be passed out and later collected each time they are used. The flow of these academic materials represents a special kind of transition and can affect the time available for instruction and practice.

Why Use Special Procedures
to Manage Classroom Materials?

There are several commonly used methods of passing and collecting materials. However, some of them cut heavily into the time scheduled for instruction or seatwork. For example, teachers may go around to each student's desk to pass or collect materials—a time-consuming procedure. Even if the teacher is giving directions to the students in the process, the method cannot be recommended. Directions given in this manner usually are ineffective; the students will not be paying as close attention as if the teacher were in front of the class. Having one student carry out the passing and collecting process may be an improvement but is still very slow.

A second common passing and collecting procedure is to ask all students to hand in or pick up their own materials. If everyone does so at the same time, it is likely to be extremely disruptive and problem behaviors (e.g., pushing, name-calling) might be triggered. Even if students do this by rows or individually, it will be somewhat disruptive and also time consuming.

A third commonly used procedure is to hand materials to the first person in each row and have students "take one and pass the rest back" or have them pass their papers to the front. Unless it is carefully monitored by the teacher, this process often leads to talking, poking, waving or dropping papers, and other disruptions.

Students can easily spend 5 to 10 minutes on one instance of passing or collecting papers. A half-dozen or more such instances a day, and the class might spend up to a half hour or an hour each day just receiving or handing in materials. Perhaps the solution to this problem lies not so much in the particular passing and collecting method used, but whether the teacher provides training and monitoring for the process. Where possible, we recommend using student helpers for passing and collecting routines, and we acknowledge the importance of training *all* students to pass and collect materials appropriately. Teachers can avoid disruptions if they have the materials ready before each activity begins, and if they teach students to carry out these tasks quickly and quietly. By planning ahead, teachers can save the minutes these activities usually take and use that time for instruction. This chapter provides several procedures for managing the flow of materials in the classroom.

Who Is Involved in Managing Classroom Materials?

The teacher, an aide (if available), volunteers, and students can all participate in the process of preparing materials to be used in class. Teachers should see themselves as planners, organizers, and supervisors of this process. The teacher is ultimately responsible for ensuring that all materials are conveniently available in sufficient quantity at the time they are needed. However, others can be involved in running off dittos; stuffing folders; stacking or sorting books, workbooks, or papers; sharpening pencils; counting out the number of materials needed; writing instructions on the chalkboard; running errands for the teacher; and so on. In fact, students are often *eager* to do these things for the teacher, and they may be given the privilege of helping as a reward for doing well in their academic work.

These same people also have roles in passing and collecting materials. The teacher can direct and supervise the actions of others while students follow the rules and expectations outlined in the next section.

Although having materials ready is the teacher's responsibility and sometimes requires considerable energy and time, Chapter 3 presents ideas for having aides, volunteers, and students assist you with the tasks.

How to Manage Classroom Materials

In this section we discuss the use of supplementary materials, the availability and storage of materials, and passing and collecting procedures. Managing the orderly flow of materials can make a difference in how quickly your students move from one activity to another and in how efficiently you use instructional time in the classroom.

Developing Supplementary Materials

Regardless of the type of instructional materials you may have in your classroom, you should probably develop a few supplementary activities before the year begins. These materials can be used to give some of your lower performing students extra practice in skills that prove difficult for them. If you invest time in modifying some of your classroom materials before the students arrive, you will find that you can use the school year more efficiently.

You can decide which of your materials may need to be modified by identifying what problems students have experienced in previous years. For example, many students find it difficult to learn "b-d," "m-n," or "p-g" discriminations. The teacher who can anticipate this and other common problems can help students overcome them by making slight modifications and nominal additions to the traditional curriculum. Several possible methods can be used to modify and supplement the texts in your classroom.

1. *Develop extra worksheets.* By providing students with more drill and practice in areas where they are having some difficulty, teachers can teach these students more efficiently. If you can anticipate which skills are likely to prove troublesome to students and develop supplemental sheets for these areas, you will be able to give students the necessary practice. Although some texts provide supplemental practice materials, they usually have two important drawbacks: (1) the practice sets are not provided for the areas in which students are experiencing difficulty and (2) even if some extra practice is provided, often it is not extensive enough to improve the skills of the low-performing student. Therefore, the materials you develop could mean the difference between academic failure and success for these students.

2. *Develop instructional games to supplement skill practice.* Students often view supplemental practice as drudgery. It may prove worthwhile, therefore, to develop a few instructional games that students will find reinforcing. These games could consist of simply providing students with a highly motivating activity that also enables them to practice necessary skills. Teachers who develop these activities before the school term starts will find that games help maximize the time spent in direct instructional activities during the school year. Development of these instructional games should follow a few simple rules.

- Keep the game construction simple (materials do not need to be elaborate).
- Gear the activity to a specific academic skill (e.g., letter-sound relationships).
- Develop the game so that one to four students can play.
- Make the game noncompetitive (i.e., everyone can win).
- Make the directions easy enough so that students can follow them with little or no teacher guidance.

3. *Make changes in the sequence of material presented in the basal program.* We have found that teachers who are not afraid to alter the sequence of skill presentation within traditional material often reduce the number of students who have trouble learning content. These changes need not be extensive. For instance, if the material presents words before students have seen all the sound/symbol relationships required to sound out the words, you could modify the sequence by skipping ahead in the text to the activities teaching those critical sounds. Three excellent books are available to guide you: *Direct Instruction Reading* (Carnine & Silbert, 1979); *Direct Instruction Mathematics* (Silbert, Carnine, & Stein, 1981); and *Theory of Instruction* (Engelmann & Carnine, 1982).

Having Needed Materials Ready

The most basic way to manage handing out and collecting materials so the process does not interfere with academic activities is to prepare all needed materials beforehand. Ways other people can help you with this advanced preparation are outlined in Chapter 3. In addition, always have extra supplies on hand of the materials students usually keep at their desks, including pencils and tablet paper. When students get caught without a sharp pencil or run out of their own paper, you can save considerable time by providing students with the needed materials immediately.

Before students go home that day, you might want to remind them to stock up on the necessary supplies, to sharpen their pencils and the like, then praise them for doing so. This could provide substantial time savings the next day and possibly avoid the disruptive effects of students borrowing supplies from their neighbors, sharpening pencils, and so on while the rest of the class waits. You might want to write yourself a note on the chalkboard to make these reminders at the day's end.

Storing Materials Conveniently

Materials and extra supplies should be stored near each instructional area. For example, the teacher's reading manual—along with charts, overheads, other teaching materials, student workbooks, readers, and necessary supplies—should be kept in the area designated for reading instruction. A bookshelf, small table, or student desk may serve as storage space if it is within easy reach while the teacher is providing instruction.

Another area must be designated for the collected work and/or materials. Monitors must be taught not only to return materials to their proper storage area, but also to store or sort collected materials that must be corrected, graded, and returned to the students. Rectangular boxes or baskets marked for each academic subject can hold collected work that needs teacher attention. These subject area boxes help organize papers for correcting and recording and avoid cluttering the teacher's desk with student work. (See Chapter 9 for procedures that make correcting papers easier and more efficient.) A separate box can be used to hold work that will be returned to students. Many students enjoy the use of "cubbyholes" or individual "mailboxes" as a means of receiving materials from the teacher.

Passing and Collecting Procedures

The five basic rules for passing and collecting are as follows:
1. Pass or collect materials quietly.
2. The paper monitors pick up the materials quickly.
3. Paper monitors pass or collect in their zone only.
4. Pass or collect without touching other people.
5. Monitors return materials to the correct storage area.

A script is provided to present these rules to the students. Twenty minutes should be allowed the first day for teaching and practicing the new procedures. This small investment of time will be repaid many times over if you follow the procedures specified. Be sure to have all necessary materials, extra student supplies, and the subject area collection boxes marked and ready before you begin. You should also have the room divided into two zones for passing and collecting.

Prepare a list of materials monitors beforehand. Students often are overly eager to help and may disrupt the class when they volunteer. For this reason it is important to choose monitors fairly and systematically through alphabetical order, seating arrangement, or a similar system. The main point is that students know when it is their turn to serve as monitor. Student monitors are expected to follow transition rules and to complete their assigned work. Otherwise, they must forfeit the privilege of being a monitor.

Once you have introduced the procedures, remember to praise students who follow the rules. Review the rules if your students do not follow the procedures or if a new student enrolls in your class.

Script for Introducing Passing and Collecting Materials Procedures

Teacher	Students
"Today we are going to learn a new way to pass and collect the materials we sometimes need to do our work."	
"It is important that we pass and collect papers quickly and quietly."	

Teacher	Students
"What is important about passing and collecting materials?" (signal)	"Pass and collect papers quickly and quietly."
"Yes, we pass and collect materials quickly and quietly. Here's how we do that. First, pass or collect materials quietly."	
"What is the first rule for passing and collecting materials?" (signal)	"Pass or collect materials quietly."
"That's right. Here's another rule. The paper monitors pick up the materials quickly."	
"What's another rule for passing and collecting papers?" (signal)	"Paper monitors pick up the materials quickly."
"Yes, you're right. The paper monitors must pick up the materials quickly."	
"Here's another rule. Paper monitors pass or collect in their zone only."	
"What do paper monitors do?" (signal)	"Pass or collect in their zone only."
"You've got it. Paper monitors pass or collect in their zone only."	
"The next rule is to pass or collect without touching other people."	
"What's the next rule?" (signal)	"Pass or collect without touching other people."
"That's right. You remembered."	
"The last rule is monitors return materials to the correct storage area. What's the last rule?" (signal)	"Monitors return materials to the correct storage area."
"Great! Let's say all five rules for passing and collecting materials."	"Pass or collect materials quietly. Pick up the materials quickly. Pass or collect in your zone only. Pass or collect without touching other people. Return materials to the correct storage area."
"Nice job!"	
"Whenever we need to pass or collect materials, I will ask two students who	

Teacher	Students
have *followed the rules* during transition time and *finished their work* to be the paper monitors for the next period."	
"How do you get to be a paper monitor for the next period?" (Call on individual students.)	"Follow the rules and finish your work."
"Super. How do the paper monitors pick up the papers?"	"Quickly."
"Yes, quickly. I'm going to show you how to pick up materials quickly." (Teacher goes to the area where materials are kept and picks them up quickly without talking.)	
"What did I do?"	"You didn't talk, you were quick, and you didn't touch anyone."
"That's really good. You remembered the rules."	
"Now I will show the zones for collecting and passing out materials." (Teacher divides room into two zones and gives them a name, e.g., color, number, description such as front and back.)	
(Teacher tests.)	
"Which zone is this?"	"Zone 1."
"Yes, Zone 1. So what zone is this?"	"Zone 2."
"Good, Zone 2."	
"Now tell where paper monitors collect or pass materials."	"In their own zones."
"That's right. In their own zones."	
"Now I will show you where the materials are stored." (It will be necessary to show different areas for different materials.)	
"Now, let's practice passing and collecting materials quickly and quietly." (Teacher picks two students who qualify to be monitors and has them practice passing and collecting.)	

Teacher	Students

"Remember, pass or collect without talking or touching. Only the paper monitors pass and collect materials. I'm going to watch while you follow the rules by not talking and not touching anyone. I'm going to see if the monitors get the materials quickly and pass only in their zones."

Managing Materials in the Classroom
Implementation Checklist

1. Are sufficient quantities of all needed materials for each instructional period ready and accessible prior to each period? Materials could include:
   - Books
   - Workbooks and ditto worksheets
   - Overheads, instructional charts, or work on the chalkboard
   - Paper
   - Pencils, pens, or chalk
   - Special supplies such as globes, maps, science equipment, or audio-visual equipment

2. Are all materials in their designated areas?
3. Have new students been trained in passing and collecting procedures?
4. Have you reviewed the rules for passing and collecting materials recently?

A Survey of Research

The ideas for this chapter were based on surveys of methods used by teachers in their classrooms rather than on research literature. We found little in the literature that addressed specific procedures or even recognized these procedures as an organizational issue. Therefore, we can only cite logic and actual classroom experiences, not literature, to support the procedures we recommend in this chapter.

References

Carnine, D., & Silbert, J. *Direct instruction reading.* Columbus, Ohio: Charles E. Merrill, 1979.

Engelmann, S., & Carnine, D. *Theory of instruction.* New York: Irvington, 1982.

Silbert, J., Carnine, D., & Stein, M. *Direct instruction mathematics.* Columbus, Ohio: Charles E. Merrill, 1981.

Chapter 8

Handling Student Requests for Assistance

A request for assistance is any attempt by the student to get help from the teacher, another adult in the classroom (aide, volunteer, or visitor), or a peer with work that has been assigned. These requests usually take the form of questions ("What's this word?"), complaints ("This is too hard"), or negative self-statements ("I can't do this stuff!").

Why Use Special Procedures to Manage Requests for Assistance?

One of the main features of elementary school education is that students frequently are expected to work by themselves on written assignments at their desks or work stations. Independent seatwork may be scheduled for lengthy periods while the teacher conducts small-group instruction, tutors individual students, or completes paperwork. Even though teachers try to match the work with each student's ability level, the pupils still may need help with their assignments.

Students often are taught to request assistance in several ways: (1) remain seated, raise their hands, and wait for the teacher to come to them; (2) approach the teacher and wait for a turn; or (3) ask a classmate for assistance. Students do not always follow these procedures. Instead, they sometimes request assistance by (1) remaining seated, but calling out; (2) approaching and interrupting the teacher, or (3) interrupting another student. Or students may simply not seek the assistance they need.

Several problems can arise when students break the rules for seeking assistance. The classroom becomes noisy and students are distracted if children talk aloud; the teacher finds it difficult to get things done if interrupted frequently; or students conversing together prevent others, and themselves, from completing their work. Those students who are not comfortable requesting help often use incorrect procedures or simply fail to complete their independent work. Yet even when the rules are followed and students wait quietly for help, valuable learning and teaching time is wasted. Students are not learning to work independently, but to "kill time" while waiting and to depend upon the teacher for help in completing their work. A wait of even a *few* minutes can mean the loss of valuable academic time.

Casual observation suggests that when students raise their hands or leave their seats to obtain help, they stop working on their assignments. Students often need two hands to work—one to hold their paper or book and one to write—and usually need to be at their desks. If they raise their hand, they generally look up as well and may remain off-task until they receive the teacher's attention. Further, the amount of time a student spends on-task is closely related to the level of learning achieved. Thus, to develop independent on-task behavior and increase their learning potential, students must be taught to request assistance nondisruptively and to work while they wait for help.

The following section describes a nondisruptive procedure for requesting assistance that also allows students to learn the efficient use of time and to develop better independent work habits.

How to Manage Requests for Assistance

Each student is given a three-sided card and a folder. The card is taped to the student's desk, and the student uses it during seatwork time to signal the teacher for help needed with assigned work. The folder contains work that the student can turn to for practice while waiting for the teacher's help.

During seatwork time, the teacher acknowledges requests for assistance and praises those who continue to work, while ignoring those who do not follow the procedure. This procedure allows students to make a "continuous" request for assistance without disrupting their work time, constantly interrupting the teacher, or bothering other students. The teacher, when free, circulates through the room, answering questions and helping those students who have displayed their cards. This monitoring activity should be entered into the daily schedule so that the teacher has time to assist students before going on to the next scheduled activity.

Constructing Assistance Cards

You can make the cards for requesting assistance from a 9 by 12-inch piece of colored construction paper or lightweight tagboard. Write on the paper with a felt-tip or other broad-point pen in letters large enough to be seen easily across the room; then laminate it to make it durable. Construct the cards and attach them to student desks with strapping tape so that they cannot be torn off easily. These directions will help you construct and attach the cards.

1. Obtain paper or tagboard, materials for lamination, a broad-point pen, strapping tape, and a stapler (optional). You will need enough ma-

terials to make one card for each student. You might want to make a few extra cards in case some students' cards become damaged or a new student joins the class.

2. Fold the paper evenly into two 4-inch sections and two 2-inch sections (see Diagram 1). Print "Please Keep Working" on one 4-inch section. This side will face the student when the card is attached to the desk. On the other 4-inch section, print "Please Help Me." This side will face out toward the teacher. (You may write different messages if you prefer.) Then laminate the paper.

Diagram 1

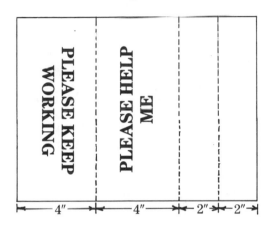

3. Next, fold the paper into a triangular shape with two 4-inch sides and a 2-inch base (see Diagram 2). Tape or staple the triangle together.

Diagram 2

4. Attach the signs with 1 1/2-inch strapping tape along the bottom edge of the "Please Help Me" (facing out) side and the outer edge of the students' desks. This allows the card to be raised or lowered easily (see Diagram 3).

Diagram 3

Card Raised   **Card Lowered**

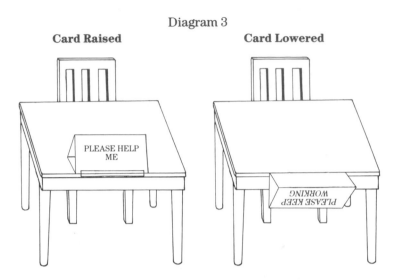

PLEASE HELP
ME

PLEASE KEEP
WORKING

Assembling "Sure-Fire" Work Folders

Students are also provided with a folder containing "sure-fire" work that can be done without teacher assistance or instruction. An example of sure-fire work might be a sheet containing practice on math facts, writing consecutive numbers to 100, or writing spelling words or sentences using spelling words. It is important that students be able to do the work without teacher assistance. It should provide meaningful practice related to current or recent academic lessons, but it should not be so intriguing that it draws students away from their regularly assigned work. For example, an entertaining short story or cartoon math sheet might be more fun than regularly scheduled work but might distract students away from their main assignments. Such materials should not be used in the folders.

The folders are made out of large sheets of construction paper measuring approximately 16 by 20 inches. The folders are labeled with students' names and have pockets inside to hold their work. Tagboard file folders may be substituted. In lieu of pockets, worksheets may be paper-clipped to the folder. Follow these instructions to construct folders:

1. Obtain construction paper (one large piece for each student in the class), a marking pen, and tape or a stapler.

2. Fold the paper in half lengthwise and cut a 4-inch slit on the fold at one end. This will give you two 4 by 10-inch tabs.

3. Fold over each of the tabs and fasten them with tape or staples to form pockets on the inside of the folder.

4. Write each student's name on a different folder along with the label *"Sure-Fire Work."*

5. Place a 1 day's to 1 week's supply of sure-fire work in each student's folder, adjusting the level of work to each student's ability. Otherwise, what is "sure-fire" for some students will be too hard or too easy for others. The best guideline is to choose work you know the student can do but could use more practice on.

Implementing the Procedure

After materials have been prepared for each seatworker, you are ready to instruct the students how and when to use the cards and folders. Tape the cards to students' desktops and have them keep the folders inside their desks with their other books and supplies. When the procedure is carefully taught and consistently carried out, students quickly learn to raise the card when they need help and to continue working while they wait by going on with their main assignment or using their sure-fire work folder. A script for introducing the use of cards and reviewing the rules for requesting help is provided at the end of this section.

The following steps will help you teach students how to request assistance nondisruptively.

1. Use the script to introduce the use of cards and model the use of the cards for the students.

2. Make sure you can see the students' cards from where you are located during small-group instruction of other activities.

3. Periodically scan the classroom to watch for students who request assistance.

4. Acknowledge students who use the card: "I see your card, John. I'll help you as soon as I can. Please keep working."

5. Scan the classroom and praise students who are working while they wait and those who are working without help: "Susan, thanks for remembering to work while you wait."

6. Ignore students who do not use the procedure.

7. For the first few days, review at the beginning of each day how to use the cards. Review every day the first week, then review when students seem to be forgetting how to use the cards, after a vacation break, or when a new student is enrolled (use the review script for this purpose).

8. Make sure at the beginning of *each* day that *each* folder has enough sure-fire work to carry the student through the day.

These procedures for requesting help are easy to teach and to implement. Students enjoy using the cards and knowing what to do when the teacher isn't free to help them. Learning to scan the classroom periodically for "help me" signs may take some practice. At first, you may want to use a cue to help you remember such as after the students you are working with read so many lines in a book or after you complete a certain number of tasks in a lesson. You might also want to put up a sign in your room reminding you to scan and praise. In the beginning stages, it may be helpful to scan at least once or twice a minute.

Remember to praise students who use their cards and continue to work. If possible, ignore students who wave their hands or approach you while you are teaching, or simply remind them of the rules for requesting assistance. You might want to provide several practice sessions for all students before implementing the procedure. This will allow you to practice scanning, acknowledging, and praising students who work while they wait for help. To do this, you can give a seatwork assignment that takes approximately as long as a small-group instructional period. You may remain seated at your instructional area or circulate through the classroom. Scan the room, acknowledging and praising those students who use the procedure correctly. After one or two practice sessions, you and your students will be ready to begin using the procedure. One final note: you can expect students to overuse their cards the first few days after the procedure has been introduced. However, the novelty quickly wears off, and students will soon begin using them only when necessary.

Script for Introducing Requesting Assistance

Teacher	Students
"Today we're going to learn a new way to ask for help when I'm working with the group or helping another student."	
"You all have a three-sided card like this attached to the front of your desk. (Show the card.) You're going to learn to use this card when you need help during my group time. One side of the card says, 'Please help me!' What does it say?" (signal)	"Please help me."
"The other side says 'Please keep working.' What does it say?" (signal)	"Please keep working."
"Whenever you need help while I'm busy, all you need to do is raise the card. The side that I see tells me you need help. The side you see tells you to keep working. What are you going to do if you need help?" (signal)	"Raise the card."
"That's right. Raise your card and keep working. Most of the time I won't be able to help you right away. The side of the card you see tells you what to	

Teacher	Students
do when I can't come. What should you do?" (signal)	"Keep working."
"Yes, keep working. Sometimes you might be stuck on a problem. When that happens just go to another part that you can do. What should you do if you get stuck?" (signal)	"Go to another part we can do."
"Yes, go on to another part you can do. (Ask children about several different situations that might come up in your classroom and what they should do in each one.) The important thing to remember is to do what the sign says."	
"What does the sign tell you to do?" (signal)	"Keep working."
"Right, keep working. Sometimes you might get really stuck and can't go on. When that happens you will use a folder like this (show folder). Inside is your "sure-fire" work that you can do all by yourself. Whenever you're really stuck you'll go to your sure-fire work and do that. What will you do when you get really stuck?" (signal)	"Do work from our sure-fire folders."
"Yes, do the work in your sure-fire folders." (Ask the children what they should do in different situations that might come up in your classroom.)	
"*Let's review*. If you need help while you are working, what should you do?" (signal)	"Raise the card and keep working."
"Yes, raise the card and keep working. What should you do if you get stuck?" (signal)	"Go on to another part or do our sure-fire work."
"What's the important thing to remember?" (signal)	"Keep working."
"Yes, keep working. Remember to use your card and keep working when you need help. Let's try the cards once before we begin work. Show me what you'll do when you need help." (signal)	(Children respond.)
"That's right. Please put your cards down and begin your work."	

Script for Reviewing Requesting Assistance

Teacher	Students
"Let's review. If you need help while you are working, what should you do?" (signal)	"Raise the card and keep working."
"Yes, raise the card and keep working. What should you do if you get stuck?" (signal)	"Go on to another part or do our sure-fire work."
"What's the important thing to remember?" (signal)	"Keep working."
"Yes, keep working. Remember to use your card and keep working when you need help. Let's try the cards once before we begin work. Show me what you'll do when you need help." (signal)	(Children respond.)
"That's right. Please put your cards down and begin your work."	

Handling Student Requests for Assistance
Implementation Checklist

1. Does each student have a "Please Help Me" sign attached to the desk? If any student does not (if it has been torn, lost, or stolen, or if the student is new to the class), make a card and attach it to the student's desk.
2. Does each student have a folder containing sufficient, appropriate sure-fire work? (Prepare them as necessary.)
3. Have you recently reviewed the rules for using the procedures for requesting assistance? (Do so, if necessary.)
4. Are you periodically scanning the room to see who needs assistance? (Cue yourself to do so, if necessary.)
5. Do you acknowledge those students who request help and praise those who work by themselves and who continue to work while they wait? (Cue yourself, if necessary.)
6. Do you ignore or reteach those students who do not follow the procedure? (Students who receive assistance when they have broken the rules probably will continue to request assistance disruptively.)

A Survey of Research

While small-group instruction has been shown to be very effective for teaching basic skills to students (Rosenshine, 1979), many teachers find it difficult to teach a group and at the same time manage the behavior of independent seatworkers. As a result, the seatworkers often become nonattentive or disruptive. On the other hand, if they need help with their assignments, they must wait until the teacher can give them directions or assistance. Very often they stop working as they wait. Since current research shows that the amount of a student's on-task time is closely related to achievement (Rosenshine, 1979), procedures for maintaining high levels of on-task behavior during seatwork are critically important.

The teacher is thus faced with a dilemma: "Should I interrupt my small group to help my seatworkers or should I let the seatworkers wait and take the chance they will stop working?" Fortunately, there is at least one solution to this dilemma.

A basic element of the solution is the use of teacher praise to sustain on-task behavior. Early research in behavior analysis showed that teacher praise is the key to effective classroom management (Becker, Madsen, Arnold, & Thomas, 1967; Cossairt, Hall, & Hopkins, 1973; Hall, Lund, & Jackson, 1968; Madsen, Becker, & Thomas, 1968). However, early research also taught us that these comments must be *contingent* on appropriate student behavior (Hart, Reynolds, Baer, Brawley, & Harris, 1968). Otherwise, some other, less appropriate behavior may be strengthened instead. Research has also shown that praising one student can influence other children nearby (Broden, Bruce, Mitchell, Carter, & Hall, 1970; Kazdin, 1973). Thus, praise appears to communicate teacher expectations and approval throughout a classroom.

However, praise alone will not maintain student attention. The solution also requires procedures that address students' occasional needs for assistance and back-up work tasks. Such procedures have been designed by Stan-Spence and Spence (Note 1) and provide the basis for this chapter. Stan-Spence and Spence worked with a classroom of youths with serious behavior problems and academic deficiencies. By sufficiently structuring the youths' environment, Stan-Spence and Spence were able to reverse many of the youths' behavior problems and to correct many of their academic deficiencies.

Paine, Rosellini, and Quintero (1980) described two studies that made use of Stan-Spence and Spence's card-and-folder procedure and teacher praise. In the first study, seatwork students in two elementary school classrooms were taught to request assistance nondisruptively and to work while they waited for help. The teacher provided cards and work folders, then scanned and praised the seatworkers while teaching a highly structured small-group lesson. Seatworkers' appropriate behavior increased markedly over baseline levels when the request and praise procedures were implemented. A side effect of the procedures in this study was an *increase* in the teacher's instructional pacing in the small group and an *increase* in her praise to group members. In the second study described by Paine et al., high school special education students learned to work more efficiently during a study period while their teacher conducted a small-group lesson. Again, praise and task structuring successfully increased students' attention to assigned tasks.

Reference Notes

1. Stan-Spence, A., & Spence, I. *Temporal structure.* Paper presented at the meeting of the Fifth Annual Convention of the Association for Behavior Analysis, Dearborn, Mich., June 1979.

References

Becker, W. C., Madsen, C. H., Jr., Arnold, R., & Thomas, D. R. The contingent use of teacher attention and praise in reducing classroom behavior problems. *Journal of Special Education*, 1967, *1*, 287-307.

Broden, M., Bruce, C., Mitchell, M. A., Carter, V., & Hall, V. R. Effects of teacher attention on attending behavior of two boys at adjacent desks. *Journal of Applied Behavior Analysis*, 1970, *3*, 199-203.

Cossairt, A., Hall, V. R., & Hopkins, B. L. The effects of experimenter's instructions, feedback, and praise on teacher praise and student attending. *Journal of Applied Behavior Analysis*, 1973, *6*, 89-100.

Hall, R. V., Lund, D., & Jackson, D. Effects of teacher attention on study behavior. *Journal of Applied Behavior Analysis*, 1968, *1*, 1-12.

Hart, B. M., Reynolds, N. J., Baer, D. M., Brawley, E. R., & Harris, F. R. Effect of contingent and noncontingent social reinforcement on the cooperative play of a preschool child. *Journal of Applied Behavior Analysis*, 1968, *1*, 73-76.

Kazdin, A. E. The effect of vicarious reinforcement on attentive behavior in the classroom. *Journal of Applied Behavior Analysis*, 1973, *6*, 71-78.

Madsen, C. H., Becker, W. C., & Thomas, D. R. Rules, praise, and ignoring: Elements of elementary classroom control. *Journal of Applied Behavior Analysis*, 1968, *1*, 139-150.

Paine, S., Rosellini, L., & Quintero, P. *Concurrent use of discrete techniques: Managing seatworkers' behavior while providing small group instruction.* Eugene, Oreg.: Direct Instruction Follow Through Project, University of Oregon, 1980.

Rosenshine, B. Content, time, and direct instruction. In P. L. Peterson & H. J. Walberg (Eds.), *Research on teaching: Concepts, findings, and implications.* Berkeley: McCutchan, 1979.

Chapter 9

Managing Paperwork: Correcting Students' Papers

Although regular written assignments are an important part of student learning, correcting students' daily work can take up a great deal of a teacher's time. This chapter presents three strategies for dealing with this potential burden—correcting as you circulate, individual self-correction, and group self-correction.

Correcting as You Circulate

One way to handle the time-consuming task of correcting papers is to correct some student work while you circulate and provide help during seatwork periods. This can be beneficial for both you and your students.

Why Correct Students' Work as You Circulate?

First, the procedure is an efficient use of teacher time. Several teachers have reported that they finish 30 to 40% of their correcting work by doing it as they circulate.

Second, it provides immediate feedback to students and can effectively reinforce their efforts. Students who know that they are on the right track are likely to work harder and to complete their work.

Third, correcting while you circulate alerts both you and the students to problems they are having before they "practice" doing a skill the wrong way over and over. For example, a teacher may notice that a student has forgotten to carry a 10 into the tens column on the first two multiplication problems of an assignment. The teacher can then remind the student about the carrying rule before the entire assignment is completed. If students practice doing something the wrong way more than a few times, it will be harder for them to do it correctly in the future. Thus, it is well worth the teacher's time and effort to monitor students' performance during work periods.

Who Is Involved in Correcting while Circulating?

Since correcting students' work can reveal valuable information about their progress and problems with the material, you, the teacher, will want to do much of the correcting yourself. You will know when to give students positive feedback and when to provide tutoring to help them correct their errors. However, an aide or a volunteer, if available, also can be trained to correct while circulating to help with the process.

How to Correct while Circulating

Correcting while circulating can be done whenever some or all of your students are doing written work at their desks and you are not teaching. The process is quite simple. Be sure to carry a pen that writes in a different color ink than the pen or pencil students use to self-correct their work (see section in this chapter on self-correction). This will allow you to tell your marks from those students make on their own papers. Also, use a pen that students cannot "borrow" so they are not tempted to mark on papers that should not be self-corrected. In addition to the pen, some teachers like to carry an answer key for the assignment students are working on, especially when they cannot easily tell whether an answer is correct (e.g., complex multiplication problems). Make sure when carrying the answer key that other students nearby cannot see it.

Begin the circulating and correcting process with your lower performing students or with those who have their "help me" cards raised. This will help ensure that those who need your assistance the most will get it before you run out of time. Then, gradually work your way around the class. When you have been with each student once, and if you still have time, start the process again. If time is limited, simply return to those students who were having trouble with their work on your first round. By this time they will have completed additional problems or items, and you can check on their progress. The process of making a second or third round in the same work period will help you determine whether the tutoring you gave them helped clear up the problem they were having. If so, you will know they are now on the right track. If not, you can use this occasion to provide additional help.

Each time you stop at a student's desk, correct at least two items—and as much as an entire row or section of items, depending on how much time you have. However, be sure to scan and praise periodically if you focus your attention for more than 15 to 30 seconds. Correct answers can be marked with a "C" (for correct), a star, or a happy face, depending on what you and your students prefer. Remember to praise the student for work done accurately. Errors can be marked with a dot, since some students get upset or discouraged if other error marks (i.e., a check mark or a minus) are used. The dot can be converted into a "C," plus mark, or other positive mark after the student has corrected the item. If you make the dot slightly larger than a single pencil mark, you can see it easily enough to gain an accurate count of how many errors students make on their first attempt. When you find an error, try to determine whether the student simply made a careless mistake or did not know how to do the item correctly. If the latter, you might need to tutor the student. Provide the tutoring immediately, and assign the same item or similar item(s) to work on next. Tell the student that you will check back in a few minutes to look over the new assignment. Be sure to follow through as promised. If several students are having difficulty with the same item, you might want to provide group tutoring or review the skill the next time you teach that subject area.

Student Self-Correction

Students can check their own papers in many subject areas. They can compare their answers against a teacher-prepared answer key, or the teacher may give the answers aloud or put them on a chalkboard while students correct their own papers.

Why Use Self-Correction Procedures?

Self-correction helps students become more independent and responsible for their own work and provides them with immediate feedback that prevents repetition of errors. Students who correct their own math problems immediately usually will not practice doing them the wrong way. However, if they have to wait a few days for the teacher to return their papers, they sometimes do more problems incorrectly before catching the error. It then takes much longer to correct the error patterns. When students check their own work, they can focus on what they do not understand and learn quickly from their mistakes. Self-correction by students also gives the teacher more time to help students who need extra tutoring.

How to Use Student Self-Correction Procedures

The first step in initiating a self-correction procedure is to establish a checking station. The checking station can be a table or several desks pushed together and must be visible from the teaching area. Set up a separate station for each subject area. Each station should have colored correcting pens for student use and teacher-prepared answer keys for the assignments to be self-corrected. There should be a box or a folder in which students can place their completed and checked work.

Rules for using the correcting station should be introduced to the students and posted at the station (see the script at the end of this section). The rules are:

1. Only one person at each answer key.
2. Leave your pens or pencils at your desk. (Only correcting pens are allowed at the station.)

3. Check your work without talking.

4. Put all corrected work in the box.

The teacher or aide monitors the use of the checking station and praises students who use it correctly.

How students self-correct

1. Students complete the assignment and "double-check" it at their desks to make sure that all items have been completed.

2. Students go to the checking station and circle any errors with the colored pen.

3. Students return to their seats to correct the errors.

4. They go to the checking station to recheck their corrections.

5. When their assignments are 100% correct, the students place them in the box for completed assignments.

6. If all the answer keys are being used, students work on another assignment while waiting to use the checking station.

How to prepare for student self-correction

1. Prepare the checking station for only one subject at first. Math is an easy subject for students to correct. Language or other subjects can be added later.

2. Post the rules at the station.

3. Introduce self-checking to students by using the script and by modeling it.

4. Set expectations for proper use of the checking station by reviewing the rules frequently with students.

- For the first week, review rules every day.
- The second week, review them every other day (M, W, F).
- In succeeding weeks, review the rules the first day of each week and when it appears that students are not following them. Also, review rules the first day after a break in the school schedule.

5. Reinforce correct checking. It is important to focus on encouraging students to find *all* their errors. Praise careful checking: "Good, you found that mistake."

6. Spot check at least some of the students' papers each day to determine their accuracy at self-correction.

Rewards and consequences for self-correction

1. Rewards should be given for correct work and correct checking. The teacher or aide should select one paper at random from among those each student has corrected to check for accurate self-correction. It is important that students have no idea which paper will be checked.

2. If a student checks a paper incorrectly, there should be a consequence. Cheating in any way could cost points, time from recess, staying after school, and the like.

3. The teacher should stress both the importance of doing a good job on assignments and checking them correctly for errors.

4. The student can earn a plus, or some other positive mark, for final accuracy on the paper if all items are properly corrected. The plus can be added to the feedback chart (see Chapter 11) toward earning activity time or some type of reward.

5. When students are checking their papers, the teacher and/or aide should always praise them for correct checking behaviors (following the rules) and for finding errors. The praise should be given frequently at first and then generally phased out when the students consistently follow the rules while checking.

Script for Introducing Student Self-Correction

Teacher	Students
"Today we're going to start correcting our own (subject area) papers a new way. As (grade) graders, you are old enough to correct your own papers. I have set up a correcting station over there." (point)	
"What am I going to ask you to do?" (signal)	"Correct our own papers."
"Watch me while I tell you how to do it." (Teacher goes through the motions while explaining.)	
"When you are done with an assignment, you leave your pencil at your desk and take your paper to the correcting station."	
"At the correcting station is a colored pen and an answer key. You check each answer with the answer key."	
"If you miss any answers, circle them."	
"Let's go over it again. Listen."	
"First, leave your pencil at your desk. What's the first thing that you do?" (signal)	"Leave your pencil at your desk."
"Right! Second, take your paper to the correcting station. What's the second thing you do?" (signal)	"Take your paper to the correcting station."

Teacher	Students

"Yes! The third thing is to check each answer with the answer key. What's the third thing you do?" (signal)

    "Check each answer with the answer key."

"The fourth thing you do is circle wrong answers. What's the fourth thing you do?" (signal)

    "Circle wrong answers."

"Good! You've got that part of it. Now listen to the last part."

"When the papers are checked, go back to your seats, cross out the wrong answers, and write in the correct answers. What do you do after you've checked your paper?" (signal)

    "Go back to your seat. Cross out the wrong answers. Write the correct answers."

"Now you're almost done. Check your paper again with the answer key. What do you do after you correct your mistakes?" (signal)

    "Check it again with the answer key."

"When your paper is all correct, put it here in the box. (Show students the box.) Where does your paper go when it's done?" (signal)

    "In the box."

"It's very important to find all your mistakes. Then, when I look at your papers, I'll know what I need to teach you. I expect you to be honest. Each day I'll look at one of the papers that you check to make sure you've checked it correctly. You won't know which paper I might check. If you find all your mistakes, you can earn a plus to put on the chart." (Use the last sentence only if using a feedback chart.)

"Here are some rules for using the checking station: first, only one person at each answer key. What's the first rule?" (signal)

    "Only one person at each answer key."

Teacher	Students
"Second, leave your pens or pencils at your desk. What's the second rule?"(signal)	"Leave your pens or pencils at your desk."
"Good. Third, check your work without talking. What's the third one?" (signal)	"Check your work without talking."
"Right. Fourth, put all corrected work in the box. What's the fourth rule?" (signal)	"Put all corrected work in the box."
"That's right. Fifth, if the station is full, do other work at your seat until there is room. What's the fifth rule?" (signal)	"If the station is full, do other work at your seat until there is room."
"These rules are posted here for reminders." (Teacher points to the rules.)	

Group Self-Correction

Group self-correction provides some of the same benefits as self-correction—efficiency, immediate feedback and practice, and detection of error patterns. An additional advantage is that the teacher knows immediately whether each student has mastered the skill.

Group self-correction can be used at the end of an instructional lesson or a supervised practice activity. The teacher leads the correction procedure while the students stay in their seats and check their papers with a colored pen.

How to Use Group Self-Correction

1. Have the answers ready to display on an overhead projector or chalkboard.

2. When all students have completed the assignment, ask them to pick up their correcting pens. Check to see that everyone has done so.

3. Uncover the first answer on the overhead or chalkboard.

4. Point to the first answer and say (for example): "Give yourself a plus if you spelled _(word)_ correctly. Circle any incorrect answers and correct them with the correcting pen."

5. Continue until all answers are checked, one at a time.

6. As with individual self-correcting, stress finding *all* mistakes.

After collecting the papers, spot-check them for accurate checking and provide consequences accordingly.

Correcting Students' Papers
Implementation Checklist

Correcting as You Circulate

1. Have you identified a time(s) when you can circulate and correct?
2. Do you have a special pen and any necessary answer keys ready?
3. Do you remember to go back and check students who were having trouble on the first round?

Student Self-Correction

1. Are the checking pens at the checking station?
2. Are the answer keys prepared and at the stations?
3. Are the checking station rules posted?
4. Have you reviewed the checking station rules with the class recently?
5. Are you praising and rewarding students who follow the rules at the checking station? Prompt yourself to do so, if necessary.

Group Self-Correction

1. Is the answer key ready to display on the overhead transparency or chalkboard?
2. Is the overhead projector set up and in position? Is the chalkboard covered?
3. Is there a checking pen for each student?

A Survey of Research

The procedures described in this chapter are based primarily on research done by Farnum and Brigham (1978). These authors investigated the effects of having elementary school children score their own study guides. Students were found to be quite accurate (93%) in scoring their own work even when no contingencies were placed on their accuracy. Further, the majority of students preferred self-scoring their assignments to having the teacher score them. No adverse academic effects of the procedure were found; students who evaluated their own work scored just as well on exams as did students whose assignments were judged by the teacher.

In a related experiment, Hundert and Bucher (1978) examined three forms of self-scoring with groups of elementary and secondary special education students. Students were found to score their work accurately both when they reported and when they did not report their scores to the teacher. However, when they received reinforcement for reporting improved scores over previous performances, they exaggerated their improvements. In reality, their actual scores remained fairly constant throughout all phases. To discourage exaggerated reporting, the authors developed a checking procedure whereby scoring accuracy was verified publicly for all students. The students received bonus points for accurate scoring and penalties for evaluation errors. Later, a streamlined version of this procedure was instituted in which the accuracy of only one student's paper, chosen at random, was checked. Both checking procedures controlled exaggerated reporting, and teachers expressed satisfaction with the considerable time savings produced by the techniques.

References

Farnum, M., & Brigham, T. The use and evaluation of study guides with middle school students. *Journal of Applied Behavior Analysis*, 1978, *11*, 137-144.

Hundert, J., & Bucher, B. Pupils' self-scored arithmetic performance: A practical procedure for maintaining accuracy. *Journal of Applied Behavior Analysis*, 1978, *11*, 304.

Chapter 10

Dealing with Behavior Problems

The classroom management plan proposed in this book is designed to prevent misbehavior through the use of positive, prestructured proce dures. But occasionally students do not respond to these preventive measures. In these instances, it may be necessary to use a mild punishment procedure.

This chapter describes how to use warnings and loss of privileges as a way of dealing with student misbehavior, that is, behavior not allowed by the classroom rules. This procedure has proven effective with most students. (Suggestions for managing the behavior of extremely disruptive students who do not respond to warnings and loss of privileges can be found in a number of other books on behavior management.)

What Is the Warning Procedure?

When a student misbehaves, you should first react by praising the appropriate behavior of other students nearby. Follow the praising guidelines provided in Chapter 4, and try to make your praise sound sincere, not accusatory. If this tactic does not work, tell the student that the behavior is not acceptable, describe the expected behavior, and warn the student of the consequences if the inappropriate behavior is continued. If the student does not respond to the warning, restate it, then take away a privilege the student has enjoyed. A student who talked during a work time would receive a warning such as "Steve, this is a warning. You need to work without talking or you will lose some recess time."

Some behaviors, such as hitting someone or name-calling, are so unacceptable that students should not be allowed to exhibit them even once without a consequence. Each teacher and school will have specific guidelines regarding such behavior. For these types of offenses, no warning is given; instead, a predetermined consequence is carried out.

Why Use the Warning Procedure?

In some situations students don't respond to suggestive praise. When this happens, you need a more direct way to deal with misbehavior. The warning serves as a mild punishment procedure and has been used effectively by many teachers.

The warning procedure is easy to implement because it requires only that a teacher notice the inappropriate behavior and speak quickly to the student about it. The procedure can be used from anywhere in the room, even while the teacher is involved in another activity. If a student needs a second warning, the teacher writes the student's name on the board. (This is described in detail in the next section.)

The warning procedure needs no extra materials. The privileges that a student may lose are usually a part of the regular school day, such as recess time. Because students value these privileges, the threat of losing them is usually enough to stop the misbehavior or reduce its occurrence.

How to Use the Warning Procedure

The warning procedure can stop many problem behaviors before they become disruptive to the class. The steps we outline here give minimum attention to the student who is misbehaving yet do not permit the inappropriate behavior to continue.

1. If a student is misbehaving, give suggestive praise to the students nearby who are exhibiting the correct behavior. If Sue is drawing a picture when she should be doing her math, an example of suggestive praise to students around her would be "John, you're going to get all your math done today," "Ellen, I like the way you're trying to do as many problems as you can." Give the praise once to two or three students, then wait about 30 seconds to see if the misbehaving student responds. If the student responds and exhibits the correct behavior, wait a few seconds, then praise that student.

2. If the student does not respond, keep a neutral and unemotional facial expression and tone of voice as you tell the student, "Sue, this is a warning. No drawing now. I want you to do your math." If possible, deliver the warning from nearby (about a meter away), as this seems to be more effective than delivering it from a distance. Establishing eye contact while giving a warning, and looking back shortly afterward to see if the student has complied, also makes a warning more effective. You should not get into a conversation with the student or give the student any more attention than is necessary to convey the warning. Praise students who are on-task to keep them from focusing attention on the student who is being warned. If the student begins the appropriate behavior at this point, wait a few seconds to a minute, then praise the student for it.

3. If the student doesn't respond to the warning, calmly say "Sue, you were given a warning about drawing. One mark," then write the student's name on the board and put a mark next to it.

Some teachers have found that certain students like the attention that comes from having their names put on the board—it singles them out. Each time a mark is added beside their names, they seem to like it more, and they soon get into a power struggle with the teacher over who is in control. When this happens, the procedure is not working and must be altered or abandoned. One alternative is to have *all* students' names posted all the time, either on the chalkboard or on 3 by 5-inch cards on the bulletin board. When a problem behavior occurs, the students' names are removed (erased or taken down). If additional marks must be made by the student's name, this can be done on a note the teacher carries on a clipboard or has at the desk. At "privilege time" only the students whose names are still posted are given the privilege.

4. If the student doesn't comply, the teacher marks another point. This should be done without comment, giving the student as little attention as possible. Continue to praise other students for appropriate behavior.

5. At this point, if the student still does not exhibit the appropriate behavior, repeat Step 4.

6. For behaviors that are totally unacceptable, predetermined consequences may be used. For example, if a student calls another student a name or hits someone, a mark may be given with no warning. You should identify these serious unacceptable behaviors at the beginning of the school year. Communicate them to your students, and make sure you carry out the consequence whenever one of the behaviors occurs.

7. Each point after a student's name stands for a loss of privileges. One point could stand for 5 minutes lost from recess, two points mean 10 minutes lost, and so on. The consequence may be the same for every child in the class or different for different students; but the point system will be effective only if students lose privileges they value. For example, if a student sometimes wants to stay in from recess, taking time away from recess will not work for that student, and you will have to use some other mildly undesirable consequence instead.

8. The student should get no extra attention when missing time from recess, staying after school, and the like. Consequences of the point system should not be reinforcing in any way.

Introduction of the Warning Procedure

The first time a student receives a warning, the teacher should explain, "This is a warning. If I have to tell you to begin work again, I will write your name on the board (or remove your name) and mark a point. Each point means that you'll lose 5 minutes of recess." This should be explained only for the first warning a student receives. It need not be explained to each student. After the teacher has explained it to three or four students, the remaining students should catch on.

Remember:

1. Try praising nearby students first.
2. Clearly say "This is a warning."
3. Use a calm voice.
4. Give the misbehaving student as little attention as possible.
5. Continue to praise others who are exhibiting appropriate behavior.
6. Make sure the student doesn't like what the points stand for.

Dealing with Behavior Problems
Implementation Checklist

1. Before school starts in the morning, erase the names and points on the chalkboard from the previous day (or put back the deleted names). You might have a student do this for you.
2. When a student engages in minor misbehavior, first praise the students sitting nearby who are working appropriately.
3. If this does not stop the misbehavior, say clearly but calmly "This is a warning . . ." Make sure you give the student as little attention as possible.
4. If the student still does not stop misbehaving, use the loss of privileges procedure described in the chapter, then withhold time from the student's next free-time period.
5. Continue to praise other students.

A Survey of Research

In spite of the general effectiveness of positive reinforcement, techniques such as praise, points, and privileges are sometimes not effective with certain students. Therefore, mild forms of punishment are sometimes necessary to eliminate problem behaviors.

Loss of privileges, sometimes called a response cost procedure, has been shown to be a powerful intervention when used in combination with praise and other reinforcers (Walker, Hops, & Fiegenbaum, 1976). For example, Walker and Hops (1976) reported that a combination of points, praise, and response cost was extremely effective in managing classroom problem behaviors, in fact, more so than using any of these variables alone.

Walker, Street, Garrett, and Crossen (1977) reported the use of a response cost system to improve the behavior of an aggressive boy on a school playground. The treatment virtually eliminated all instances of aggressive and socially negative behavior. The effects seemed to carry over during playground periods when the response cost procedures were not in effect.

Negative attention (verbal reprimands) has also been investigated. Forehand, Roberts, Doleys, Hobbs, and Resick (1976) demonstrated that negative attention reduced the incidence of noncompliance, whereas repeated commands to a student had little impact. In another experiment, these same authors showed that when negative attention, time-out, and ignoring were compared, each procedure was effective in modifying noncompliance; however, the negative attention procedure was associated with increased on-task behavior.

Several studies have investigated the effect of how reprimands are given. For example, a study by O'Leary, Kaufman, Kass, and Drabman (1970) demonstrated that a teacher's loud reprimands actually *increased* the disruptive behaviors of an entire first grade class, while soft reprimands reduced them. Interestingly, the quiet reprimand had a similar effect as praising, that is, appropriate behavior increased when the procedure was implemented.

Van Houten, Nau, MacKenzie-Keating, Sameoto, and Colavecchia (1982) found several characteristics that influence reprimand effectiveness. In one study, reprimands delivered with eye contact and a "firm grasp on the student's shoulders" were found to be more effective than those delivered without these characteristics. In a second experiment, physical proximity to the student being reprimanded was shown to be important. Reprimands delivered from 1 meter away were more effective than those given from a distance of 3 meters.

A third experiment conducted by Van Houten et al. revealed a "spillover effect" occurring with reprimands. That is, reprimands delivered to one member of a student pair decreased the disruptiveness of both students. This finding suggests that reprimands tend to have a general quieting effect. If the message is delivered publicly, it can communicate to other students in the room that misbehavior will not be tolerated. However, the effectiveness of reprimanding will be reduced if the teacher does not take advantage of the quiet moments in the classroom to praise appropriate behavior. If teachers rely only on negative attention (reprimanding), they will soon find themselves caught in a criticism trap (see Chapter 4).

A final warning about overreliance on behavior reduction techniques (e.g., warnings, point loss, reprimands) comes from McLaughlin and Malaby (1972). These authors found that point loss for misbehavior in an intermediate classroom was only somewhat effective until the teachers awarded points for quiet behavior. Then inappropriate behaviors decreased substantially. This finding suggests that behavior reduction procedures, while they seem to be the most natural approach to classroom management, have only limited potential and may even backfire, as in the criticism trap. Only when procedures to increase positive behavior are combined with those to decrease negative behavior do teachers achieve the best results in the classroom.

References

Forehand, R., Roberts, M., Doleys, D., Hobbs, S., & Resick, P. An examination of disciplinary procedures with children. *Journal of Experimental Child Psychology*, 1976, *21*, 109-120.

McLaughlin, T., & Malaby, J. Reducing and measuring inappropriate verbalizations in a token economy. *Journal of Applied Behavior Analysis*, 1972, *5*, 329-333.

O'Leary, K., Kaufman, K., Kass, R., & Drabman, R. The effects of loud and soft reprimands on the behavior of disruptive students. *Exceptional Children*, 1970, *37*, 145-155.

Van Houten, R., Nau, P., MacKenzie-Keating, S., Sameoto, D., & Colavecchia, B. An analysis of some variables influencing the effectiveness of reprimands. *Journal of Applied Behavior Analysis*, 1982, *15*, 65-83.

Walker, H., & Hops, H. Use of normative peer data as a standard for evaluating classroom treatment effects. *Journal of Applied Behavior Analysis*, 1976, *9*, 159-168.

Walker, H., Hops, H., & Fiegenbaum, E. Deviant classroom behavior as a function of combinations of social and token reinforcement and cost contingency. *Behavior Therapy*, 1976, *7*, 76-88.

Walker, H., Street, A., Garrett, B., & Crossen, J. *Experiments with response cost in playground and classroom settings*. Eugene, Oreg.: Center for Research in the Behavioral Education of the Handicapped, University of Oregon, 1977.

Chapter 11

Developing Good Work Habits: The Feedback Chart

The feedback chart is one kind of point system used in classroom management. It may be used to provide the teacher with information about how each student is doing in four areas related to successful classroom behavior. Students' performance throughout the day is posted publicly on this chart. Initially, this is done for each academic period in the school day. Later, use of the chart can be phased out gradually as student performance remains at a consistent level.

The chart has the students' names down the side and the academic periods across the top. In constructing the chart, the blocks for the subject areas should be left blank and filled in each day, since the schedule may vary each day. Each block is divided into four sections (see Figure 11.1).

Figure 11.1
Feedback Chart

	Math	Reading	Language	
Alison				
Debbie				
Fritz				
Joe				
Marty				
Pat				
Eric				

These sections are used to record student behavior with respect to (1) correct transition time, (2) work done at an acceptable accuracy level or following the directions of the group, (3) work completed or working the whole time, and (4) no more than one warning for misbehavior (see Figure 11.2A).

Figure 11.2
Sample Recording on Feedback Chart

A

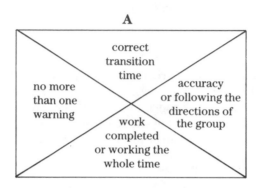

B

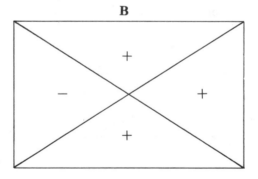

Figure 11.2B shows that a student went through a transition time correctly, completed the work, worked at an acceptable level of accuracy, but received more than one warning for misbehavior.

The chart should be posted where all students can see it and where the teacher can reach it easily. Once made, the chart should be laminated so that it is erasable and can be used repeatedly. The feedback chart will provide useful information about student performance to teachers and students alike. The plusses that a student earns can be traded for participation in an activity period at the end of the day.

Why Use a Feedback Chart?

There are several important reasons why a feedback chart may be included in this program, if desired. First, it provides students with a visual display of their daily progress. The teacher directs student attention to the chart throughout the day through the use of praise and by posting the plusses when the entire group is watching. Examples of directing students' attention to the chart through the use of praise would be "John earned all his plusses for two periods in a row," "So far today, Jill completed every assignment." Second, research indicates that public posting of students' performance increases work completion and accuracy.

Third, it is an easy way to collect valuable data to help make educational decisions for students. For example, if a student receives minuses each day for work completion, the teacher will be alerted to the problem and can find out why the student is not completing assignments. Is more time needed? Is the student off-task? Does the student need to be praised more during this time to work faster? Is the student unable to do the work? By evaluating the information on the chart, the teacher can then devise ways to help this student complete the work. Some teachers have shown these charts to parents at conference times. A feedback chart can be valuable in improving student performance in many areas.

How to Use the Feedback Chart

First, you or an aide must make the chart. Draw it on tagboard with a felt-tip pen, then laminate it for repeated use. A transparency pen should be kept available nearby for marking the chart. Post the chart in an easily accessible and visible spot, and introduce it with the script that appears at the end of this section. Be sure to have on hand a list of possible activities for the special activity period when you use the script.

Once you have introduced the chart, begin marking points at the end of each period while the whole class watches. As an alternative, have an aide, volunteer, or student mark the points while you call out whether each student gets a plus or a minus. First mark whether each student completed the assigned work (plus for complete, minus for incomplete). To know this, you will have to collect the papers and look quickly at each one as you mark the points. If the students are not expected to finish a work assignment until later in the day, you will have to wait to mark the work completion points for that assignment until after the later work period. For a seatwork assignment that may take several periods to complete, a plus can be earned for working the whole time. Make sure you let students know at the beginning of the period what is expected of them. For example: "To earn your plus, this worksheet must be all done" or

"You have enough math in your folders to last all week. To earn your plus you must work the whole time. I need to see your pencil moving and your eyes looking at your paper the whole time." The teacher will need to look up and scan several times a minute to monitor this (see the monitoring and praise procedures described in Chapter 4).

You will also mark whether each student received one warning or less, or more than one, during the period (a plus for one warning or less, a minus for more than one). You can keep track of these warnings on the chalkboard (see Chapter 10).

As you mark the points, call attention to them as in the following example: "It's time to mark our points." (Read down the chart as quickly as possible.) "John did all his work, no warnings." (Teacher marks two plusses quickly.) "Adam, work done, no warnings."

When transition time occurs, stand by the chart, watch students, and mark a plus or minus for each one. Make sure a student does all four transition time behaviors correctly before awarding a plus for the transition. Announce these points as you give them.

At some point in the day (as soon as papers are corrected), fill in the plusses or minuses for work done with an acceptable level of accuracy. These points can be announced at this time or just before the special activity period. Papers can be checked through student self-correction or correction by a teacher or teacher aide (see Chapter 9). The accuracy level is to be determined by each teacher. In general the accuracy level should be set (1) slightly higher than students are currently achieving, (2) at a level that students have the ability to reach *most* of the time, and (3) high enough to encourage students to perform to their maximum ability. There may be some periods in which students are not expected to complete a written lesson, for example during oral math practice or a lesson such as Distar Language. In these cases, award a plus for following the directions given to the group. Make sure that you state the directions to the group clearly.

Set aside a short time (no more than 10 minutes) at the end of each day to add up the points earned by each student and to conduct an activity period as a reward for those students who have earned a prerequisite number of points. Calculate the requisite number of points by taking 90% of the total possible points for that day. Make a criterion chart like the one illustrated here to post for handy reference.

Number of Periods	1	2	3	4	5	6	7	8
Possible Points	4	8	12	16	20	24	28	32
Points Needed for Activity Period	3	7	10	14	18	22	25	29

For example, if today there had been four academic periods, it would have been possible to earn 16 points. Each student would have needed at least 14 points (approximately 90% of 16) to participate in the day's special activity.

Remove those students from the group who have not earned activity time and have them put their heads down and sit quietly, continue their day's assignments, or do other studying. Encourage them to try again tomorrow, and point out specifically what each one can do to improve.

With those who have reached criterion, conduct the earned activity. A "spirited" academic game is a good choice because it increases student learning time, using reinforcement time to practice review material. Since the activity often requires some planning, it should be selected at the beginning of the day. It may be chosen either by the teacher or by the students from among several alternative activities the teacher names. The activity should vary each day so that students do not lose interest, and should be something that will (1) cost no money, (2) require minimal planning, and (3) be something the students are willing to work for. A list of possible activities is provided in Appendix B.

Record each day's data from the chart onto a ditto copy. This task could be done by an aide or even a student. The information can be used to check on student progress and identify problem areas.

The Good Behavior Game

A technique called the Good Behavior Game can be used to add additional interest to the feedback chart. In this technique, the class is divided into teams. A team can consist of a row of students, the right half of the classroom, all of the boys, or the entire classroom if competition is to be arranged with another class. Once the teams are established, they compete to see which one can earn the most points on the feedback chart in a day. You can arrange daily competitions for the teams and keep a running tally of scores like the "standings" in baseball or basketball leagues. You can also institute "feedback chart tournaments" as a further incentive. Such arrangements may not be needed to maintain your students' interest in the chart, but they can be used periodically when their interest seems to be fading.

The Good Behavior Game underscores the importance of each point (i.e., work completion, work accuracy, no warnings, smooth transitions) for each student and often boosts students' interest in these behaviors. The game is usually effective for the same reasons the feedback chart is effective—it sets criteria for performance, provides public feedback about performance, and awards positive consequences for the winners.

If students are competing primarily against a criterion (a point goal) and only secondarily against each other, they all can end up winners in the game. Still, the inter-student competition—even if only secondary—seems to help build students' enthusiasm for the procedures. If you are not comfortable having the students compete against each other, you might encourage them to top their own personal best scores or to try for "perfect scores" several days in a row.

These and other variations of the procedure you may develop will help maintain student interest in the feedback chart behaviors for a long time—perhaps even until the behaviors are so well established that you can begin phasing out the chart.

Script for Introducing the Feedback Chart

Teacher	Students
"Today we're going to start something new. It's a new way to track how well you're doing in class."	
"We're going to keep track of four things: • If you do transition time correctly; • If you finish your work (or work the whole time); • If your work is correct (or if you follow the directions of the group); • If you get no more than one warning."	
"What are the four things we're going to keep track of?" (Call on individual students.)	"If we do transition time correctly." "If we finish our work (or work the whole time)." "If our work is correct (or if we follow the directions of the group)." "If we get no more than one warning."
"That's right. You could earn four plusses in a period if you do all four of those things."	
"At the end of the day, there will be a special activity period for every person who earns enough plusses."	
"What can you work for?" (signal)	"The special activity period."
"When will the special activity period be?" (signal)	"At the end of the day."

Teacher	Students
"You can tell how many points you need by looking at this chart." (Show students the criterion chart for determining plusses needed.)	
"If we have _____ periods in the day, then you would need _____ plusses to do the special activity."	
"If we have three periods in the day, how many plusses would you need?" (signal)	"10"
"Here is a list of things we could do during the special activity period." (Read the list to the students.)	
"If you think of anything you'd like to add, let me know."	
"Today we are going to mark points during (math, reading, language, art, etc.)."	
"Since there will be _____ periods, how many points will you need to earn the special activity period today?" (signal)	"_____"
"If you do not earn enough points for the special activity period, you will have other work to do."	
"What four things can you earn plusses for?" (Call on individual students.)	"Doing the transition time correctly." "Finishing our work." "Doing our work correctly." "Getting no more than one warning."
"What can you do if you earn enough plusses?" (signal)	"The special activity."
"What will you do if you don't earn enough plusses?" (signal)	"Other work."

Script for Reviewing the Feedback Chart

Teacher	Students
"Remember that you're working to earn plusses for a special activity period."	
"What four things do you have to do	

Teacher	Students
to earn plusses?" (Call on individual students.)	"Do transition time quickly and quietly." "Get our work done." "Do our work right." "Get no more than one warning."
"That's right. Today we'll mark plusses during (name the periods for that day)."	
"So how many plusses do you need to earn a special activity period?" (signal)	(Students look at chart.) "_____"
"Right."	

The Feedback Chart
Implementation Checklist

1. Is the chart posted where it can be easily seen and reached? Is it erased from yesterday?
2. Is there a transparency pen nearby to mark the chart?
3. Is the activity for the day planned or are the options selected to be voted on?
4. Are materials ready for the reinforcing activity, if any materials are needed?
5. Have you recently reviewed the four behaviors to be recorded with the class?

A Survey of Research

The feedback chart described in this chapter is quite similar to the performance feedback system described in the literature by Van Houten and his colleagues (Van Houten, 1979; Van Houten, Hill, & Parsons, 1975; Van Houten & Van Houten, 1977). Van Houten's system typically makes use of instructions, feedback, public posting of student performance, and praise to motivate students to do their best in school.

Research literature contains several instances of the effective use of performance feedback. Van Houten, Morrison, Jarvis, and McDonald (1974) described its use to increase the volume and quality of student writing in second and fifth grade students. Similarly, Van Houten, Hill, and Parsons (1975) used feedback to increase story writing performance in fourth graders and to promote a variety of reading and language exercises with fifth graders. An analysis of this intervention found timings, feedback, posting, and praise to be the effective elements.

Performance feedback has also been used successfully in special education (Van Houten & Van Houten, 1977). This study revealed the importance of publicly posting students' scores rather than communicating them privately, and showed that feedback systems often tend to generate considerable discussion among classmates regarding their successes. Van Houten (1979) reported that the effects achieved through performance feedback systems can persist over time, a finding which supports their use.

The technique has also been effective in improving the academic performance of secondary school students (Van Houten & Lai Fatt, 1981; Van Houten & MacLellan, 1981; Van Houten & McKillop, 1977). For a comprehensive overview of performance feedback procedures with various student groups and target behaviors, see Van Houten's book, *Learning Through Feedback* (1980).

Like Van Houten's performance feedback system, our feedback chart procedure includes several working elements: it places contingencies on both academic and conduct behaviors; it sets criteria for acceptable performance in both areas; it provides feedback to students on how their behavior matches the teacher's expectations; it calls for public posting of student performance scores; and it provides rewards (activities) for meeting the expressed criteria. In addition, classroom rules and the teacher's praise become part of the procedure. One element of the performance feedback system that does not appear in our description of the feedback chart is the use of timing as a motivational device. Although timing is not described as part of this chapter, it can certainly be used with the feedback chart, as Van Houten discusses in his book and articles. We also provide some guidance for the use of timings in Chapter 6.

The Good Behavior Game described in this chapter is also taken from research literature. While it often focuses on student conduct, it also can be played using academic performance, in which case it resembles the performance feedback system. Harris and Sherman (1973) analyzed the components of the Good Behavior Game and found that its effectiveness seemed to be determined by dividing the class into teams, setting a criterion for winning, and providing back-up consequences for the winners. However, Harris and Sherman found only a slight improvement in academic behavior when the game focused on students' conduct. This finding suggests that teachers should provide direct rewards for academic success and add incentives for conduct as needed.

It should be remembered that the feedback procedure is fairly complex and sophisticated, and its effectiveness depends on many variables. If the procedure is not working for you, it may be that one or more of the steps is not being given careful attention and is working against your objective. For example, public posting—potentially a powerful variable—will not be effective if students' attention is never directed to the posted scores or to what they mean. By adjusting how you administer the system, you should be able to find some form of the intervention that will again motivate your students to improve their conduct and academic performance.

References

Harris, V., & Sherman, J. Use and analysis of the "Good Behavior Game" to reduce disruptive classroom behavior. *Journal of Applied Behavior Analysis*, 1973, *6*, 405-417.

Van Houten, R. The performance feedback system: Generalization of effects across time. *Child Behavior Therapy*, 1979, *1*, 219-236.

Van Houten, R. *Learning through feedback: A systematic approach for improving academic performance*. New York: Human Sciences Press, 1980.

Van Houten, R., Hill, S., & Parsons, M. An analysis of a performance feedback system: The effects of timing and feedback, public posting and praise upon academic performance and peer interaction. *Journal of Applied Behavior Analysis*, 1975, *8*, 449-457.

Van Houten, R., & Lai Fatt, D. The effects of public posting on high school biology test performance. *Education and Treatment of Children*, 1981, *4*, 217-226.

Van Houten, R., & MacLellan, P. A comparison of the effects of performance feedback and sentence-combining instruction on student t-unit length. *Education and Treatment of Children*, 1981, *4*, 17-33.

Van Houten, R., & McKillop, C. An extension of the effects of the performance feedback system with secondary school students. *Psychology in the Schools*, 1977, *14*, 480-484.

Van Houten, R., Morrison, E., Jarvis, R., & McDonald, M. The effects of explicit timing and feedback on compositional response rate in elementary school children. *Journal of Applied Behavior Analysis*, 1974, *7*, 547-555.

Van Houten, R., & Van Houten, J. The performance feedback system in the special education classroom: An analysis of public posting and peer comments. *Behavior Therapy*, 1977, *8*, 366-376.

Chapter 12

Phasing Out the Special Procedures

So far in this book we have discussed how to organize classroom space, rules, and roles; described procedures for managing time, materials, requests for assistance, and paperwork; and suggested ways of managing the classroom through attention, feedback, and warnings. If you apply these procedures and follow the guidelines outlined, you can achieve major changes in the organization and management of your classroom.

The primary goals of this effort are to develop a classroom that runs as smoothly and efficiently as possible, to build a positive and encouraging learning environment for students, and, as a result, to have students work hard and learn as much as possible. The special procedures described in this book have several characteristics in common: they focus on systematic structures and consequences for behavior; they emphasize positive approaches; they are highly planned and organized; and, when used as described, they work. However, they cannot be continued indefinitely. The final step in creating a successfully structured classroom is to phase out many of the special procedures.

Guidelines for Phasing Out Special Procedures

A special procedure should be phased out when it adds greatly to your workload, keeps students dependent on an artificial structure, or differs substantially from the procedures that students will experience the next year. In this program, phasing out is required for the following: the management of transition time, the use of the feedback chart, and the rate at which students are praised. Note that we are not suggesting you eliminate praising completely—only that you cut back on how often you praise. Your continued praising, even though it will occur less often, is essential to continued good student performance. It reminds students that you are continuously aware of what they are doing and that you notice their efforts to do well.

Several other procedures—setting rules, managing materials, and managing requests—will remain in effect. You can phase out the process of *communicating* these procedures to the students by shifting from the

151

introductory script to regular use of the *review* script (when provided) for 2 or 3 days, then to *occasional* use of the review script after breaks of more than 2 days.

Still other procedures (organizing space, involving others, managing paperwork, and using warnings) will not need to be altered after their introduction. They are primarily procedures to help you organize and operate the classroom and will not make students overly dependent or create difficulties for them when they move to other classrooms. Table 12.1 provides an overview of the procedures, showing which should be phased out and which should be retained.

Table 12.1
**Overview for Phasing Out
and Retaining Program Components**

Component	Phase-Out Procedures	Criteria for Beginning Phase Out
Organization of space	None; continue procedures	
Involvement of others	None; continue procedures	
Classroom rules	Continue procedures, but reduce your praise rate for following rules	Continue full procedures at least 1 month, then begin to phase out following the first week with no more than one violation of classroom or transition time rules
Managing time	Discontinue *announcing* transition times (review as necessary); continue scheduling and timing procedures	
Managing materials	None; continue procedures	
Managing requests	None; continue procedures (review as necessary; praise occasionally)	
Managing paperwork	None; continue procedures	
Praising	Continue procedures, but reduce your praise rate	Praise at a high rate, at least 3 to 4 times a minute, while supervising seatwork for the first week; then twice a minute for the first month; then phase out in stages until the rate is once in 10 minutes after the first month

Component	Phase-Out Procedures	Criteria for Beginning Phase Out
Feedback chart	Phase out as described in this chapter	Continue full procedures for 1 month, then phase out after the first week in which 95% of your students meet the 90% point goal on 5 consecutive days
Warnings	None; continue procedures	

Why Phase Out the Special Procedures?

Phasing out the special procedures is critical for several reasons.

1. Students may need to depend on specialized techniques to help them learn appropriate behavior at first. However, if students continue to rely on such procedures *when they no longer need them*, they will not do well in other situations in which they have new teachers or less structure. As a result, you need to phase out the specialized procedures so that students will learn how to respond to a variety of situations. Special procedures are a *teaching* tool. Often these special procedures are used to help students perform appropriately when they have had problems in school or have not yet learned how to make the most of their school experience. Once students are performing well, however, the procedures should be phased out gradually so that students learn to work independently in less structured situations and to respond to the directions and rewards that are part of all classroom environments. Students who already do so are often called "intrinsically motivated." They seem to work for no apparent reward other than the completion of their classroom assignments or the "joy of learning." Most students can be taught to work for these "natural rewards."

2. Students need to learn how to manage their *own* behavior. When you gradually eliminate specialized procedures, you are teaching students to take greater responsibility for themselves. They will begin to look for and go after the rewards that are intrinsic in learning itself and which are not necessarily provided by a teacher.

3. You want students' positive work habits to continue indefinitely. Once school behavior is consistently positive and strong, it is maintained best by unpredictable, "surprise" rewards and by natural rewards. You can phase out the ones students have come to expect.

When to Phase Out Special Procedures

It is desirable to begin phasing out the special procedures as soon as students' behavior is consistent for at least 2 weeks. While phasing out can be individualized, this approach is often difficult to handle. Thus, if one student still needs specialized procedures but the others are ready to have them phased out, you might wait a few days to see if the student can catch up to the others. Or, you may want to divide the class and continue specialized procedures only for those who still need them. Although it is important to begin eliminating procedures when students are ready, it is equally important to continue providing special assistance to those who still need it.

Words of Support and Caution

Procedures for phasing out are not difficult; however, they are based upon complex principles of human behavior. As a result, you will need to handle the process with care. If it is done correctly, as described in the next section, students will continue to do well for fewer rewards. You can expect minor deterioration in *some* behavior of *some* students. The phase-out rules tell you what to do if you see students regressing. It is important to follow the procedure carefully. Changing the plan or skipping steps could jeopardize its effectiveness. The guidelines have been developed to maximize your chances for success with the students.

Steps for Phasing Out the Special Procedures

Usually 3 to 6 weeks after implementing the special procedures, your classroom should be running smoothly as students become accustomed to the various rules and structures. You can then begin to phase out the procedures according to the nine-step plan described in Table 12.2 at the end of this section. Phasing out can be accomplished on the basis of "successful days," that is, days in which students observe all the rules of a procedure during the phasing-out time. For example, if you are phasing out transition time and one or more students misbehave when moving from one activity to another, that day should not be considered a successful phase-out day. You will need to repeat the same step in the plan the following day.

When you begin the phasing-out process, check the plan at the beginning of each day or during your planning time. Follow the instructions for Step 1 of the plan. If students handle themselves well during all transitions that day, cross off Day 1 on the chart and work for a second consecutive successful day. If the second day is also successful, move to Step 2 the following day. If Day 2 is not successful, go back to Step 1 until you achieve 2 consecutive successful days. If you have difficulty meeting this criterion, review the full procedure for managing transition time described in Chapter 6, then initiate the phase-out plan again. Continue to follow this strategy, marking off successful days as they are achieved and staying at the current step or backing up as necessary, until you have worked your way through the entire phase-out plan.

At best, if students never have an unsuccessful day during the phase-out period, completing the plan will require 43 school days, or about 9 weeks. However, in most cases students will have a few unsuccessful days, so you should expect the plan to take closer to 10 or 11 weeks. If you start the procedures after the first 3 to 6 weeks of school, you can complete the entire phase-out plan between Week 15 and Week 21. This will take you beyond the December holidays and into January in most schools. However, since you could be halfway through the phase-out plan by early to mid-January when the students return from their extended winter vacation (in most districts), they may have forgotten some of the classroom procedures. Thus, for the first day or two, you might want to bring back some of the structure you had in place just before the vacation. You should then be able to return quickly to the point where you left off in the phase-out plan before the winter break.

Continue the previously described procedures for each of the other steps in the phase-out plan. Within a few weeks, your students should be behaving appropriately on their own.

Table 12.2
Phase-Out Plan

Step	Plan	Successful Days Required
1	**Transition Times**	1
	a. Remind the students of the transition time rules the first thing in the morning.	2
	b. Remind the students of the rules immediately before any *two* transitions during the day.	
	c. Praise appropriate behavior during *all* transitions. Put transition points on the feedback chart in the usual manner.	
	d. Continue procedures for all other components.	
2	**Transition Times**	1
	a. Remind the students of the transition time rules the first thing in the morning.	2
	b. Praise appropriate behavior during *all* transitions. Put transition points on the feedback chart in the usual manner.	
	c. Continue procedures for all other components.	
3	**Transition Times and Teacher Attention**	1
	a. Praise appropriate behavior during *all* transitions. Put transition points on the feedback chart in the usual manner.	2
	b. Continue procedures for all other components.	

Step	Plan	Successful Days Required
4	**Transition Times, Teacher Attention, and Feedback Chart** a. Praise appropriate behavior at the *end of the day* only. Put transition points on the feedback chart in the usual manner *but do not say anything to the students* about their transitions when you do it. b. Continue the procedures for all other components.	1 2
5	**Feedback Chart and Teacher Attention** a. At the end of *each* period, when it is time to record points, tell the class: "I'm going to record points now, but I'm going to do it privately. Watch me." Be sure the *entire* class is quiet and watching. Tell them: "I will tell you at the end of the day who has earned enough points to participate in any special activities we have." b. Make a small chart that looks exactly like the one you placed on the wall to record points. Keep the new chart on your desk. Do *not* show it to the students. c. Right before the special activities period at the end of the day, tell the students: "Everybody listen. I'm going to tell you who has earned activity time." Then read off the names of the students who earned enough points. d. Then, conduct the activity. e. Continue procedures for all other components.	1 2
6	**Feedback Chart and Teacher Attention** a. Continue recording points privately on your small chart. Do *not* tell the students you are recording points. (If the students ask about the points, tell them you are *still* recording points. Tell them you will talk about it at the end of the day.) b. Conduct the special activity period the same way you did at Step 5 — read the points out loud, read the names of the students earning the activity, and do it. c. Continue procedures for all other components.	1 2
7	**Feedback Chart and Teacher Attention** a. Continue recording points privately on your small chart. b. In the *morning*, tell the students: "Now we're going to do something new. You will have the opportunity to earn a longer special activities period. You will also be able to do some new activities during that time. What new activities would you like to include during the special activities period?" Call on individual students who have suggestions. List each suggestion on the board *if* it is an activity that can be completed in 20 minutes, and *if* you are willing to include it. Then	1 2 3 4 5 6

Step	Plan	Successful Days Required
	tell the students: "These are new activities you can do during the special activities period. (Read the list.) Remember, it will be a *longer* period. To earn it, you must have enough points for *2* days in a row. If you have enough points for *2* days, you will earn the *longer* period."	
	c. At the end of the day, read the points to the class. Circle the points of those students who earned enough points for the first day. Tell students: "These people earned enough points today. (Read the names.) If you earn enough points again tomorrow, you will have earned the new, longer special activities period." (Remember—give rewards *only* after *2* days and only to those students who earned enough points on both days.	
	d. Continue procedures for all other components.	
8	**Feedback Chart and Teacher Attention**	1
	a. Continue recording points privately.	2
	b. In the *morning*, tell the students: "Now we're going to	3
	do something new. You will have the opportunity to	4
	earn some very special rewards. You could earn (for	5
	example) a popcorn party, extra P.E. time, extra	(reward)
	recess time, or an apple-bobbing party. What else	6
	would you like to earn?" Write each student suggestion	7
	on the board *if* it is an activity you would be willing to	8
	let them do. Tell the students: "These are new	9
	activities you can do during the special activities	10
	period. Most students don't get to do these things at	(reward)
	school. To earn them, you'll need enough points *all*	11
	week. That will be hard, but I think you *can* do it. It's	12
	the kind of thing that older students do. *If* you work	13
	hard all week, you *will* have enough points by Friday."	14
	c. Do *not* read the points to the students. If they ask	15
	about their points, tell them you are *still* recording	(reward)
	them, and will talk about points on Friday.	
	d. On *Friday*, read the names of the students who have enough points. Conduct a new special activity.	
	e. Continue procedures for all other components.	
9	**Feedback Chart and Teacher Attention**	1
	a. Quietly *stop* recording points. Do *not* tell the students	2
	about this. If they ask, tell them you will talk about	3
	it on Friday.	4
	b. If you feel the students as a whole, or several	5
	individual students, did very well all week, give them	6
	the Friday special activities period.	7
	c. Give them *surprise* special activities periods. Switch	8

Step	Plan	Successful Days Required
	the special activities days around. Make it a surprise	9
	so they never know when one is coming up. Have a	10
	special activity about once every week at first, then	Continue until
	once every 2 weeks, then once a month.	the end of the
	d. Continue procedures for all other components.	school year.

Three things to remember during phase-out:

1. Keep on praising.

2. If you see students not doing well for 2 days, back up one step.

3. Continue all other program components (those not being phased out) until the end of the year.

A Survey of Research

Researchers have argued consistently for the use of phase-out procedures to help maintain changed behavior for many types of learners (Kazdin, 1975; Kazdin & Bootzin, 1972; Koegel & Rincover, 1977; Walker, 1979). Experimental data document the power of these procedures to achieve continued successful performance of newly learned behaviors.

Greenwood, Hops, and Walker (1977) examined the differential effects of three maintenance strategies after specialized instructional procedures had promoted successful school behavior. Students with whom phase-out techniques were used performed significantly better after 9 weeks than they had initially. Resnick, Forehand, and Peed (1974) gradually eliminated specialized teaching cues until they were similar to cues provided in typical teaching programs. Children who received the program performed significantly better than did a control group who did not receive the techniques.

Additional phase-out effects have been found by Timm, Strain, and Eller (1979), who examined the differential effects of response-dependent and independent phasing-out strategies. After social interaction skills were taught to socially isolated preschoolers, specialized procedures were phased out differentially. Phasing out that was based on the children's responses produced continued strong performance, while independent, arbitrary phasing did not. Response-dependent phasing has been an effective component in maintenance packages outlined by Greenwood, Hops, Delquadri, and Guild (1974) and by Hops, Guild, Fleischman, Paine, Street, Walker, and Greenwood (1978).

Data have further documented the specific positive effects of gradually reducing amounts of teacher praise, attention, and reinforcement. Koegel and Rincover (1977) taught imitation and instruction-following behaviors to autistic children using a continuous reinforcement schedule. When responses were firm, children received different degrees of reinforcement phase-out. Those receiving the greatest amount continued responding the longest after all reinforcement had been stopped. Similar results were reported by Kazdin and Polster (1973). These authors taught two mildly retarded subjects to engage in social interaction on a continuous reinforcement schedule. One subject then received a reduced, intermittent schedule. Subsequently, when no reinforcement was available, only the subject who received intermittent reinforcement continued responding.

Phasing-out strategies have received additional inferred support from follow-up data frequently presented by researchers. Phase-out of program components was part of a maintenance procedure implemented by Walker, Hops, and Johnson (1975). Koegel and Rincover (1974) phased out specialized techniques systematically to teach autistic children to work in small-group instructional settings typically found in regular classrooms. Russo and Koegel (1977) applied consequences to the behavior of an autistic child in a regular classroom and then phased out special procedures and phased in the regular teacher. Hundert and Bucher (1978) taught adolescents to report their own behavior accurately, then slowly reduced reinforcement to an intermittent, unpredictable schedule and observed continued responding. Phasing out artificial structure appears to be important for long-term student success.

References

Greenwood, C. R., Hops, H., Delquadri, J., & Guild, J. Group contingencies for group consequences in classroom management: A further analysis. *Journal of Applied Behavior Analysis*, 1974, *7*, 413-425.

Greenwood, C. R., Hops, H., & Walker, H. M. The durability of student behavior change: A comparative analysis at follow-up. *Behavior Therapy*, 1977, *8*, 631-638.

Hops, H., Guild, J. J., Fleischman, D. H., Paine, S., Street, A., Walker, H. M., & Greenwood, C. R. *PEERS: Procedures for establishing effective relationship skills*. Eugene, Oreg.: CORBEH, Center on Human Development, University of Oregon, 1978.

Hundert, J., & Bucher, B. Pupils' self-scored arithmetic performance: A practical procedure for maintaining accuracy. *Journal of Applied Behavior Analysis*, 1978, *11*, 304.

Kazdin, A. E. *Behavior modification in applied settings*. Homewood, Ill.: The Dorsey Press, 1975.

Kazdin, A. E., & Bootzin, R. R. The token economy: An evaluative review. *Journal of Applied Behavior Analysis*, 1972, *5*, 343-372.

Kazdin, A. E., Polster, R. Intermittent token reinforcement and response maintenance in extinction. *Behavior Therapy*, 1973, *4*, 386-391.

Koegel, R. L., & Rincover, A. Treatment of psychotic children in a classroom environment: Learning in a large group. *Journal of Applied Behavior Analysis*, 1974, *7*, 45-59.

Koegel, R. L., & Rincover, A. Research on the difference between generalization and maintenance in extra-therapy responding. *Journal of Applied Behavior Analysis*, 1977, *10*, 1-12.

Resnick, P. A., Forehand, R., & Peed, S. Prestatement of contingencies: The effects on acqui-
sition and maintenance of behavior. *Behavior Therapy*, 1974, *5*, 642-647.

Russo, D. O., & Koegel, R. L. A method of integrating an autistic child into a normal public-
school classroom. *Journal of Applied Behavior Analysis*, 1977, *10*, 579-590.

Timm, M. A., Strain, P. S., & Eller, P. H. Effects of systematic, response-dependent fading and
thinning procedures on the maintenance of child-child interaction. *Journal of Applied
Behavior Analysis*, 1979, *12*, 308.

Walker, H. M. *The acting-out child: Coping with classroom disruption*. Boston: Allyn and
Bacon, 1979.

Walker, H. M., Hops, H., & Johnson, S. M. Generalization and maintenance of classroom
treatment effects. *Behavior Therapy*, 1975, *6*, 188-200.

Appendix A

Visitors' Guidelines for Observing in the Classroom Structured for Success

The form in this appendix can be used by visitors to your classroom as an orientation and feedback form. We have found that teachers often spend a considerable amount of time responding to the various adults who enter their classrooms on any given day. Since your classroom, once structured for success, will be a strikingly calm and productive place, visitors will want to know something about how you achieve such good results with your students. The form helps explain how the classroom is organized, and provides space for visitors' comments.

The form in this appendix is merely a sample; feel free to alter it to suit your needs. Once you have developed a version of the form you like, keep copies in a box or folder by the door. When visitors come in, you can merely ask them to take a copy of the form to read and use as they observe, then place the completed form in another box or folder before they leave. Thus, you will not be distracted from your work with the students, visitors will learn something about your program, and you may receive valuable comments on the way your classroom functions. If desired, you can arrange to meet with your visitors outside of class or to talk with them by phone.

Using this simple form, or one like it, will help your visitors see you as an open, organized, and successful teacher—a reputation any of us would be happy to have.

Guidelines for Classroom Observation

Name _____

Affiliation _____ Date _____

Welcome to our classroom. Some of the activities you observe here may be different from those in other classrooms you have visited. This is a classroom *structured for success*, that is, a preventive, whole-class approach to classroom management. It is designed to prevent many of the problem behaviors that might otherwise occur in the classroom and uses a variety of procedures and positive consequences. While this approach involves the whole class rather than focusing on individual students, it does not mean that individual differences and needs are overlooked. There remains considerable room to accommodate various student learning rates and preferences. However, the procedures focus on structuring success for all class members and for all class components that make up a routine day.

Please use this guide as you observe student and teacher behaviors in this classroom. The guide will help you focus on the key preventive management procedures used, and your comments will provide me with valuable feedback. Before you leave the classroom, please return this form to me or leave it in the designated spot. Thank you for any input or feedback you can provide.

I will be happy to talk with you outside of class to answer any questions you may have. Please feel free to call me at _____. The best times to reach me are _____. Thank you for your interest. We hope you will visit us again.

	Yes	No	Did Not Observe
A. The use of *praise* is a positive way to manage classroom behavior.			
1. Teacher states student's name and behavior being praised.	_____	_____	_____
2. Teacher praises academic behavior.	_____	_____	_____
3. Teacher praises on-task behavior.	_____	_____	_____
4. Teacher praises socially approved behavior (being nice to others).	_____	_____	_____
5. Teacher praises often.	_____	_____	_____
6. Teacher praises other students while working with individuals.	_____	_____	_____

	Yes	No	Did Not Observe

B. Cards are used to *request assistance*; students can continue to work while they wait, which maximizes students' time on-task.
1. Teacher acknowledges cards: "I see your card." _____ _____ _____
2. Students continue to work while they wait. _____ _____ _____
3. Teacher assists students as quickly as possible. _____ _____ _____

C. *Transition time* is the time it takes to change what you are doing. Students are taught how to change what they are doing quickly and quietly to maximize time spent on academics.
1. Students move quietly. _____ _____ _____
2. Students put books away and get ready for next activity. _____ _____ _____
3. Students move chairs quietly. _____ _____ _____
4. Students keep their hands and feet to themselves. _____ _____ _____
5. Teacher praises students for correctly following rules. _____ _____ _____

D. Suggestive praise combined with a mild consequence is used to *deal with misbehavior*.
1. Teacher first praises other students who are exhibiting correct behavior. _____ _____ _____
2. Teacher clearly states, "This is a warning." _____ _____ _____
3. If misbehavior continues, teacher puts name and point on board. _____ _____ _____
4. For every point on board, student loses a privilege (e.g., access to academic game, reading time in library, chance to be line monitor). _____ _____ _____

E. Research has shown that *point systems* can positively manage student behavior.
1. Teacher marks points immediately after transition time. _____ _____ _____

	Yes	No	Did Not Observe

2. At end of period teacher marks points for receiving no more than one warning. ___ ___ ___

3. Teacher directs student attention to point chart when posting points. ___ ___ ___

4. Students need 90% of total points for day to participate in activity at end of day (e.g., academic game, "free" reading time, peer, or cross-age tutoring). ___ ___ ___

F. Students *correct some of their own work* to receive immediate feedback and focus on their errors.

   1. Students leave pencils at their desks. ___ ___ ___

   2. Students are quiet at correcting station. ___ ___ ___

   3. Students come back to seats to correct errors. ___ ___ ___

   4. Students work while they wait if correcting station is full. ___ ___ ___

   5. Students file completed papers in box or basket at station. ___ ___ ___

   6. Students go on to next assigned activity. ___ ___ ___

G. Rules are posted to inform teachers, students, aides, volunteers, and others of important classroom contingencies so that rules may be applied and followed consistently.

   1. Rules are posted so that they are clearly visible. ___ ___ ___

   2. Rules are stated positively (e.g., "Stay in your seat" instead of "Do not leave your seat"). ___ ___ ___

   3. Students follow rules. ___ ___ ___

   4. Teacher applies rules consistently for all students. ___ ___ ___

H. Desks that are arranged in straight, evenly spaced rows minimize unnecessary student interaction.

   1. Desks are arranged with adequate spacing to allow teacher to circulate around room and to monitor student progress. ___ ___ ___

	Yes	No	Did Not Observe
2. Desks are arranged so teacher can see all students.	___	___	___
3. Desks are arranged so students can see teacher and chalkboard.	___	___	___

I. Certain time-related criteria are essential for student learning: sufficient time must be allotted for academic instruction and practice, and the schedule of allotted time must be followed. Public posting of a time-efficient schedule helps the teacher and students adhere to the schedule.

	Yes	No	Did Not Observe
1. Schedule is posted where teacher and others can see it easily.	___	___	___
2. Teacher adheres to schedule.	___	___	___
3. If teacher does not follow schedule, more time is spent on academic activities than on nonacademic activities.	___	___	___

Comments on the structure or procedures used in this class

_____

_____

_____

_____

_____

_____

_____

_____

_____

_____

_____

_____

_____

Appendix B

Reinforcement Ideas Suggested and Evaluated by Teachers and Students

The following two lists of potential student reinforcers have been evaluated by teachers. An initial list of 91 possible reinforcers was suggested by one teacher, and the list was then sent to approximately 15 teachers we believed to be skilled in teaching and motivating students. We asked them to rate each item on the list of potential reinforcers as either "educational" or "not educational." Ten teachers responded to our questionnaire—all of them respected by their supervisors, fellow teachers, and other colleagues as outstanding instructors. We believe their responses, summarized on the following pages, provide valuable lists of student reinforcers.

We have also included two lists of reinforcing activities suggested and rated by 60 grade school students, and a short list of additional reinforcement possibilities.

Potential Educational Reinforcers
1. Choose a partner to work with on one project. (Check with the teacher.)
2. Help correct papers.
3. Learn how to run, or run, the movie projector.
4. Write a nice note about yourself to have your teacher read.
5. Play a 5-minute game of hangman with the teacher, class, or another student.
6. Go to the library for 5 to 10 minutes.
7. Learn a new word that no one else in the class will know. (If the teacher knows a foreign language, a word from the language could be taught.)
8. Read a story to a student in a lower grade.
9. Have an upper grade tutor (student) listen to you read.
10. Have the teacher read a short story or poem to you or your class.
11. Make a class phone book or get phone numbers from class members and write them on a card for the teacher.

167

12. Have the teacher write you a message in a code for you to figure out.
13. Choose a spelling bee for the whole class.
14. Race the teacher in an addition, subtraction, multiplication, or division fact test.
15. Visit another room for one subject. (The teacher arranges it.)
16. Have the teacher show you something interesting in the encyclopedia.
17. Have the teacher figure out how many words a minute you read. See if you can top it.
18. Listen to the record player or tape recorder for 5 minutes.
19. Look at some of the teacher's books.
20. Take an imaginary globe or map trip. (The teacher makes up a story about the place you choose.)
21. Use the yardstick or meter stick to measure things in the room for 5 minutes.
22. Get 5 more minutes to finish an assignment.
23. Have the teacher describe a science experiment you can do at school or home.
24. Write a story about your classmates.
25. Get 5 minutes of the teacher's time, uninterrupted.
26. Have the teacher choose a book for you or with you at the library.

Potential Noneducational Reinforcers

1. Use a stopwatch for 5 minutes.
2. Cancel one assignment. (Check with the teacher.)
3. Run an errand.
4. Have the teacher send a nice note home about you.
5. Get 5 minutes of extra recess.
6. Use the glitter. (The teacher shows how to use it for "first-timers.")
7. Have 5 minutes to talk to a friend.
8. Sit by the teacher during a story.
9. Get a colored star.
10. Get a stamp or a sticker.
11. Use the felt-tip pens, colored pencils, or colored chalk.
12. Get 5 minutes of free time.
13. Get to go to lunch early.
14. Play with clay.
15. Draw.
16. Pass back papers.
17. Be the line leader.
18. Make a paper airplane to fly three times.
19. Have a race with another student or the teacher.
20. Have the teacher write a nice note and send it to the principal or another teacher.

21. Choose to have the whole class eat in the room for lunch.
22. Play tic-tac-toe with the teacher for 5 minutes.
23. Get three cards (3 by 5 inches, 4 by 6 inches, etc.) for your own use.
24. Write or draw on the chalkboard for 5 minutes.
25. Color a picture.
26. Get a handshake from the teacher. (The teacher can have the student choose the type.)
27. Work at the teacher's desk or somewhere else for 5 to 10 minutes.
28. Cut stars, dolls, circles, or other designs out of construction paper or tissue paper.
29. Sharpen all the teacher's pencils.
30. Get a special bookmark from the teacher.
31. Make a pencil holder for your desk.
32. Get a small box from the teacher.
33. Make something to put on the bulletin board.
34. Take a 5-minute walk with the teacher.
35. Choose to have the whole class have a painting period.
36. Have the teacher give you a secret message for no one else to read.
37. Make a mask out of a paper bag.
38. Tell a story or jokes to the class for 5 minutes. (The teacher should preview this.)
39. Make "Happy Face" cards to pass out to the class.
40. Draw a funny picture of your teacher.
41. Cut out pictures from magazines and paste them together to make funny pictures.
42. Choose one picture from the teacher's stock of magazine pictures. (The teacher cuts out many pictures from magazines.)
43. Have the teacher pat you on the back (or give you a hug) three times during the day.
44. Have the teacher give you a big sheet of butcher paper.
45. Have the teacher (or a student) hide and you try to find him or her.
46. Be excused to go home first.
47. Have the teacher tell you the answer to one problem or question.
48. Eat lunch with the teacher.

Sample Reinforcers and Their Ratings by Students

Sixty intermediate grade students were given a list of reinforcers and asked, for each item, whether they would like to earn it as a reward.

	Yes	No
1. Look at some of the teacher's books.	13%	87%
2. Use a stopwatch for 5 minutes.	25%	75%
3. Listen to the record player or tape recorder for 5 minutes.	72%	28%
4. Choose a partner to work with on one project. (Check with the teacher.)	76%	24%
5. Help correct papers.	72%	28%
6. Get 5 minutes of the teacher's time, uninterrupted.	37%	63%
7. Learn how to run, or run, the movie projector.	55%	45%
8. Use the yardstick or meter stick to measure things in the room for 5 minutes.	20%	80%
9. Play a 5-minute game of hangman with the teacher, class, or another student.	70%	30%
10. Get 5 more minutes to finish an assignment.	53%	47%
11. Make something to put on the bulletin board.	57%	43%
12. Learn a new word that no one else in the class will know. (If the teacher knows a foreign language, a word from the language could be taught.)	45%	55%
13. Take a 5-minute walk with the teacher.	32%	68%
14. Read a story to a student in a lower grade.	50%	50%
15. Have an upper grade tutor (student) listen to you read.	22%	78%
16. Make a class phone book or get phone numbers from class members and write them on a card for the teacher.	42%	58%
17. Have the teacher write you a message in a code for you to figure out.	60%	40%
18. Choose a spelling bee for the whole class.	57%	43%
19. Race the teacher in an addition, subtraction, multiplication, or division fact test.	30%	70%
20. Have the teacher describe a science experiment you can do at school or home.	62%	38%
21. Write a story about your classmates.	30%	70%
22. Visit another room for one subject. The teacher arranges it.	43%	57%
23. Have the teacher show you something interesting in the encyclopedia.	23%	77%
24. Have the teacher choose a book for you or with you at the library.	28%	72%
25. Have the teacher figure out how many words a minute you read. See if you can top it.	55%	45%

Reinforcement Ideas Suggested by Students

To obtain these responses, 60 fourth, fifth, and sixth grade students were asked to name five things they would like to earn in school for good work. Their answers, arranged in the order of the frequency with which they were mentioned, are summarized below. Numbers in parentheses indicate how many students mentioned each reward. The preliminary list produced by student responses has been edited to organize the information, to eliminate repetition, and to sort out reinforcement ideas we could not endorse (non-nutritious food items, expensive objects, and requests running counter to the purposes of schooling—a week off from school, no more homework, etc.). This list merely suggests ideas for reinforcers for students. The numbers do not mean that *all* students will work for extra recess or that more students *wouldn't* work for something at the bottom of the list. To see how an idea goes over with the students in your class, try it out.

1. Extra recess (37)
2. More free time in class (33)
3. Prizes/rewards (24)
     Stickers (e.g., stars, seals)
     Happy notes
     Pencils
     A ruler
     A book
     "Grab bag"
     Paper
     Medals and trophies
     Certificates
     Ribbons
     A spelling reward, a math reward
     A "Student of the Week" award
4. Field trips (24)
     Skating
     Horseback riding
     Swimming
     Berry picking
     Traveling to another city
5. Games in class (19)
6. Class parties (e.g., popcorn party) (16)
7. Movies (11)
8. More time for sports (11)
     Softball
     Football

       Basketball

       Soccer

9. Structured P.E. class (more gym or P.E.) (10)
10. Free activity in gym, free P.E. time (7)
11. Get out of school early (e.g., 5 minutes) (5)
12. Extra art period (5)
13. A report card/good grades (5)
14. Eat lunch in the classroom (2)
15. Learn how to be even better at a certain subject (2)
16. A chance to help out at school (e.g., help correct papers) (2)
17. A chance to help out in the preschool as a volunteer (1)
18. A chance to teach a small reading group (1)
19. Math and other kinds of homework (1)
20. Multiplication fact test (1)
21. More spelling (1)
22. Extra math paper (1)
23. Track and field meet awards (1)
24. A chance to do a play in school (1)
25. Special things in gym class (1)
26. A gymnastics show (1)
27. More time to read library books (1)
28. A chance to run the movie projector (1)
29. A pat on the back (1)
30. A handshake (1)
31. A big hug (1)
32. Applause (1)
33. A "nice work" note from the teacher (1)
34. Time to visit, time to talk with one classmate (1)
35. Less of something we do not like (1)
36. Bringing a hamster (or other small pet) to school (1)

Additional Reinforcement Possibilities

1. Use the paper punch for 5 minutes.
2. Use three sheets of construction paper.
3. Get five paper clips for yourself.
4. Erase the chalkboard.
5. Collect the papers for an assignment from your classmates.
6. Write a note to your favorite teacher and take it to him or her.
7. Get a piece of string.
8. Wash your desk or a table off.
9. Have the teacher write you a note to call home. (The teacher monitors the call.)

10. Get to walk around the room blindfolded for 5 minutes.
11. Get two envelopes for your own use.
12. Get time to clean your desk out.
13. Cut out a cartoon strip from the newspaper, cut off the speaking balloons, make your own speaking balloons, and paste them back on the cartoon strip. (Hang it up on the bulletin board.)
14. Use the teacher's big scissors for 5 minutes.
15. Get two rubber bands to put around your papers (of your own choosing).

About the Authors

Stan C. Paine received his Ph.D. from the University of Oregon in 1978. He has been a program consultant with the Center at Oregon for Research in the Behavioral Education of the Handicapped (CORBEH), a project manager with the Direct Instruction Follow Through Project at the University of Oregon, and a post-doctoral research associate with the Early Childhood Institute at the University of Kansas. Currently he is Adjunct Assistant Professor of Education at the University of Oregon and serves as president of the Association for Direct Instruction. He is co-editor of *Direct Instruction News*, associate editor of *Education and Treatment of Children*, and co-author of several articles, chapters, and manuals on effective educational practices.

JoAnn Radicchi is a special education teacher in the Portland, Oregon, Public Schools. After receiving her M.Ed. in Special Education from the University of Oregon in 1980, she taught for two years at the American school in Katmandu, Nepal. In Nepal, she used components of this book with an international class of first graders. JoAnn is currently using the entire program with a self-contained academic needs class of third, fourth, and fifth graders.

Lynne C. Rosellini received an M.Ed. in Special Education from the University of Oregon in 1980. Since that time, she has been a teacher at Larchmont Diagnostic Center in Tacoma, Washington, where she uses this program with students who have serious learning and behavior problems. She also trains other teachers in these procedures and in use of the Direct Instruction Model through her work as an educational consultant.

Leslie Deutchman received her undergraduate training at the University of Vermont and has done graduate work at the University of Oregon. She has experience as a classroom teacher of regular, gifted, mildly handicapped, and multi-handicapped students and has served as a consultant to state and private educational agencies.

175

Craig B. Darch received a Ph.D. in Special Education from the University of Oregon in 1982. He began his career as a classroom teacher of mildly handicapped students and is now Assistant Professor of Rehabilitation and Special Education at Auburn University. He has conducted research on many of the procedures discussed in this book and currently is Associate Editor for Research for *Direct Instruction News*.